Contents

Baboon on the moon   **3**

Sir Skylight   **13**

Zoot Scoot Boogie Woogie   **23**

Information foldout   **32**

Cover illustration by John-Paul Early

A catalogue record for this book is available from the British Library

Published by Ladybird Books Ltd
80 Strand London WC2R 0RL
A Penguin Company

4 6 8 10 9 7 5 3

© LADYBIRD BOOKS LTD MM

Baboon on the moon

by Mandy Ross
illustrated by John-Paul Early

introducing the common spellings of the
long **u** sound, as in moon, few and blue

June the baboon wanted to go to the moon.

She tried to get there on a moon scooter.

Toot, toot!

Off I scoot!

Boom! The scooter blew up.

Next, June tried to swoop to the moon in a big blue balloon.

Soon the balloon came down.

Then June the baboon got some Groovy Zoom Boots.

Zoom Boots

She swooped and
she looped,

as she fl**ew** round the m**oo**n.

So here on the moon is
June the baboon.

Skylight

by Mandy Ross
illustrated by Cecilia Johansson

introducing the common spellings of the
long **i** sound, as in high, lie and sky

This is Sir Skylight. He's a shining white knight.

He is brave in the daytime,

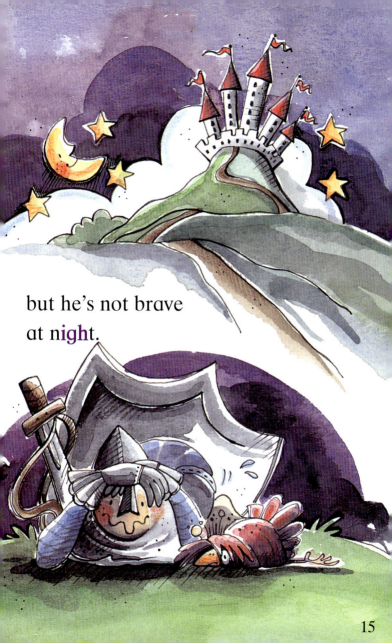

but he's not brave
at night.

He fights with all his might when there is sun and lots of light.

Yet he flies home in fright whenever
it is night.

Sir Sky**ligh**t's mum comes to tuck
him up t**igh**t,

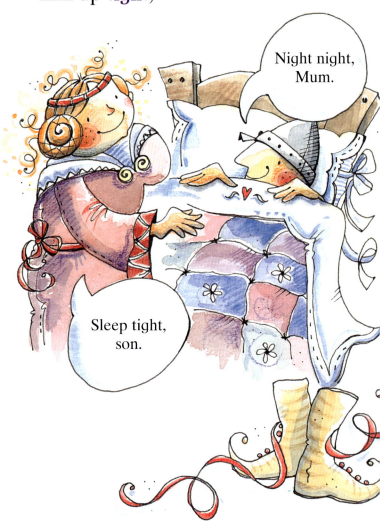

but he lies and he sighs and he cries
all night.

Then Sir Skylight has a bright idea...

"I'll be alright at night with these nice bright lights," he says.

So now when the moon
shines brightly
in the sky,

Sir Skylight rides round
with his head held high.

Zoot Scoot Boogie Woogie

by Mandy Ross

illustrated by Stephen Holmes

to practise the common spellings of
the long **a** **e** **i** **o** and **u** sounds

The animals are on the move
with a hurry and scurry.

Jake Sn**a**ke and **Wa**yne Wh**a**le t**a**ke the tr**ai**n.

We're on our way! Hurray!

Peter Cheetah pushes Neil Seal in his green wheelbarrow.

Mike Tiger and Kyle Crocodile
ride their sky-bike.

Now we're flying!

Joan Goat and Joel Mole go
by rowing boat.

June Baboon and
Sue Kangaroo use their
Groovy Zoom Boots.

The animals all hurry and scurry, for today is the day they are going to play…

in the Zoot Scoot Boogie
Woogie Animal Band!

phonics
Learn to read with Ladybird

phonics is one strand of Ladybird's **Learn to Read** range. It can be used alongside any other reading programme, and is an ideal way to support the reading work that your child is doing, or about to do, in school.

This chart will help you to pick the right book for your child from Ladybird's three main **Learn to Read** series.

Age	Stage	Phonics	Read with Ladybird	Read it yourself
4-5 years	Starter reader	Books 1-3	Books 1-3	Level 1
5-6 years	Developing reader	Books 2-9	Books 4-8	Level 2-3
6-7 years	Improving reader	Books 10-12	Books 9-16	Level 3-4
7-8 years	Confident reader		Books 17-20	Level 4

Ladybird has been a leading publisher of reading programmes for the last fifty years. **phonics** combines this experience with the latest research to provide a rapid route to reading success.

The fresh, quirky stories in Ladybird's twelve **phonics** storybooks are designed to help your child have fun learning the relationship between letters, or groups of letters, and the sounds they represent.

This is an important step towards independent reading – it will enable your child to tackle new words by 'sounding out' and blending their separate parts.

How **phonics** works

- The stories and rhymes introduce the most common spellings of over 40 key sounds, known as **phonemes**, in a step-by-step way.

- Rhyme and alliteration (the repetition of an initial sound) help to emphasise new sounds.

- Coloured type is used to highlight letter groups, to reinforce the link between spelling and sound:

and the King sang along.

- Bright, amusing illustrations provide helpful picture clues, and extra appeal.

How to use Book 9

This book introduces your child to the common spellings of the long **u** and **i** vowel sounds. The fun stories will help her* begin reading words including any of the several spelling patterns that represent these sounds.

- Read each story through to your child first. Having a feel for the rhythm, rhyme and meaning of the story will give her confidence when she reads it for herself.

- Have fun talking about the sounds and pictures together – what repeated sound can your child hear in each story?

- Help her break new words into separate sounds (eg. m-oo-n) and blend their sounds together to say the word.

- Some words, such as 'come', 'move' and even 'the', can't be read by sounding out. Help your child practise recognising words like these so that she can read them on sight, as whole words.

NEW

Baboon on the Moon and Sir Skylight

Talk about the highlighted letter groups – these represent the common spellings of the long u and i sounds, as outlined on the title-page of each story. Unusual long vowel spellings (such as in 'through') are left unmarked, as are instances of the 'magic e' spelling pattern, covered in detail in Book 7.

Zoot Scoot Boogie Woogie

This story offers your child a chance to revise all five of the long vowel sounds, in the various spellings introduced in Books 7, 8 and 9.

The text applies equally to girls and boys, but the child is referred to as 'she' throughout to avoid the use of the clumsy 'he/she'.

KV-514-015

leeds 2004

www.itchyleeds.co.uk

Editorial
Editors – Kim Whatley & Catherine Quinn

Contributors
Dan Benton, Valerie Chan, Jaimini Karsan,
Tim Marshall, Chris Marshall, Ben Moore-Bridger

Photography
Lucy Jackson, Liz Sharkey, Barbara Chapman, Nathan Emmerich,
Alex Hulme, Lauren Geisler, Gemma DeCourtney
Generic drinking shots *Matt Smith*

Team itchy
John Emmerson – North Commercial Manager
Sharon Evans – Accounts & Human Resources
Gayle Hetherington – Online Editor
Emma Howarth – Editor
Ruby Quince – Publisher
Tristan Simpson – Computers
Simon Smith – Midlands Commercial Manager
Luci Smallwood – Assistant Editor
Mike Waugh – Head of Publishing
Kim Whatley – Listings Editor
Andrew Wood – Publisher
Matt Wood & Louisa Addison – Design and Production

Thanks – All previous editors and contributors
* 07779 134984

www.itchycity.co.uk

itchy Ltd
Globe Quay Globe Road Leeds LS11 5QG
t | 0113 246 0440 f | 0113 246 0550

Whitehorse Yard 78 Liverpool Road London N1 0QD
t | 020 7288 4300 f | 020 7359 9611

e | all@itchymedia.co.uk
www.itchycity.co.uk

ISBN: 1-903753-54-6

itchy and **Fiesta**

... round and about in Leeds

Bargain caffs and flashy bistros, designer shopping and market banter, proper boozers and clubs galore, lounge bars and flash pads… we've got all you'll need here to make the most of Leeds life… and then some.

A metaphorical high-five is definitely in order for our trusty Fiesta and we like to think it feels the same. There's been fun on the roads and a new discovery at every corner… yep, we've turned this city upside down to bring you itchy Leeds 2004…

Our roll call of comedy moments for Leeds 2004

Being the butt of the joke at the HiFi comedy night – we'll never heckle again

Bumping into Chris Moyles four times in one night out on the town

Being accosted by a horde of bikini wearing blokes at Baja/Bondi – who can remember, it's all a blur

Taking our back street knowledge to new levels with the Fiesta at the fore

Old men telling us we don't know we're born at Whitelocks – a fine pint of ale and banter for free

An unmentionable incident involving an Indian waiter and a plant pot

All this and more for 2004

Beyond the call of duty – itchy and Fiesta are up for anything

Ford**Fiesta**

contents

Introduction   **5**
Introduction | Two Hours & Two Days
Days Out

Restaurants   **10**

Bars   **34**

Pubs   **54**

Clubs   **64**

Gay   **76**

Shopping   **80**

Entertainment & Culture   **96**
Live Music | Theatre | Cinema | Comedy
Museums | Art Galleries | Sports
Out Of Leeds | Entertainment Venues

Living   **112**

Body   **120**

Accommodation   **124**

Laters   **128**

Useful Information   **130**
Travel | Useful Numbers | Takeaway

Map & Index   **140**

Recommendations and other useful bits of knowledge...

Fancy Food 11
Eat Late 14
Cheap Eats 16
Outdoor Drinking................................ 41
Proper Boozers 55

Playing Pool 57
Bars With DJs..74
Cheap Drinks/Happy Hours 77
Celebrity Spotting Leeds Style 102

For sale. £345,000.

Fine glass of Chateau Musar at Norman. Staggeringly close to stunning penthouse loft in period building bang opposite Victoria Quarter. Vast, flexible living space on 2 floors with exposed brickwork, original beams and a gallery Tarzan could swing from. No wine cellar required.

LS¹ **city apartments** life agents, not estate agents

t 0113 2344111 e contact@ls-1.co.uk www.ls-1.co.uk LS1 2 cherry tree walk, the calls, leeds LS2 7E

Welcome to Leeds...

The north of England's finest city... rock up for boozing, dining, shopping, clubbing, a touch of culture and plenty of cricket. Leeds we salute you.

Leeds – officially the unofficial capital of the north. Well, the 2001 Census reckon it has the third largest population after London and Birmingham with 24,000 more birds than blokes. And Leeds blokes, on average, have the largest manhoods in Europe… must be something in the water.

As is inevitable, things they are ever-a-changin'. In the last year funky café bar Moderno closed its doors for the last time (boo), as did Brannigans (result!). The financial district saw new bars Prohibition, The Living Room, Park, Mononi and Firefly arrive, and Soul Kitchen changed into hip hangout Baby Jupiter, while the Springbok changed its name to The Barracuda Bar, as if it somehow improved the place… Finally, swanky new bar/restaurant Sandinista arrived with bells on while Bar 38 closed its doors to join the rest of the social no-hopers in the sky.

Across town, RPM, the club formerly known as the Fruit Cupboard became… erm… the Fruit Cupboard again and SpeedQueen

moved from The Warehouse to The Peephouse, and er, back again. A spangly new Bar Risa landed, with fellow newcomer The Comedy Store, and Headingley just got busier and better. To the relief of the city's music lovers, the Leeds Festival was granted a licence after last year's toilets-on-fire fiasco.

The Areas…

Call Lane/Corn Exchange – Full of hairdo beautiful folk on one side, goth teens and sk8ter bois on the other.

Northern Quarter – Light on venues, but nonetheless home to some of the best (and worst) bars in the city.

Millennium Square – Cracked paving stones, 10ft golden owls, a few bars, some restaurants and the odd club.

Financial District – Plush hotels, swanky restaurants, funky bars and lapdancing joints full of accountants.

Headingley – Home of Yorkshire cricket and rugby, 25 million students, and a transit van of burglars.

Hyde Park – Overflow area for housing the students that can't squeeze into Headingley.

Chapel Allerton – Up and coming 'village' area, favoured by young professionals.

Two Hours and Two Days in Leeds...

Two hours, two days – so many places to go in so little time. Join **Fiesta** & **itchy** on the ultimate journey through Leeds' finest. One hell of a challenge but if we can take it, you can.
Buckle up and get to it...

Two Hours In Leeds

A damn shame you can't grace this fair city for a bit longer. After that bound-to-be-hellish train/bus journey you'll need a drink to get your legs moving. Head to Revolution for some beer and a vodka chaser or Brodick's in the Corn Exchange for a swift coffee. If skatewear, bonsai trees and rare 12" vinyl aren't your thing, go flash some cash in The Victoria Quarter where you can pick up some unique clobber. If the smell of newly pressed garments brings on your shopping rage head to The Elbow Room for a few frames of pool, or to the Craft Centre and Design Gallery to browse some local art and pick up some souvenirs. Just before you head back to the station grab a bite at Maxi's Express, or if time's pressing, grab a New York style sandwich at the City Deli nestled in the station itself.

Two Days In Leeds

Stay – Radisson SAS, in the Headrow's Light Complex, is one of Leeds' nicest hotels. It's also slap bang in the centre of it all.

Shop – The Victoria Quarter is the place for decent designer clobber, as is neighbouring Harvey Nics. The Corn Exchange has some funky gifts, and Ark or DrumLoop are good places to sidle into.

Attractions – The Henry Moore Institute and City Art Gallery are right on your doorstep, as is Ster Century Cinema if you fancy a flick. For adventure further afield, head to the station and catch a train deep into the Yorkshire Dales for a hearty pub lunch and stroll around. For some sporting action, catch some rugby or cricket at Headingley Stadium.

Eat – The Calls Grill is one of the best British eateries Leeds has to offer, as is neighbouring Pool Court at 42 or The Mill Race in Kirkstall. For more exotic fare, Shogun Teppen-Yaki is a good bet, as is Thai Edge or The Olive Tree, Rodley. For ultimate stylish dining, call in at the flashy Malmaison Brasserie.

Drink – Cool bars are one of Leeds' main attractions – head down to the Call Lane bars to hang with the trendy set. Mojo is not to be missed, neither are Mook or Northern Quarter staple North Bar. For traditional Yorkshire bitter consumption, check out city centre boozers The Angel or Whitelocks or Headingley favourites The Original Oak or The Headingley Taps.

Club – Baja Beach Club is the place for sampling some of Leeds' cheese, but for a more civilised night out, The HiFi Club and its programme of funk, soul and jazz definitely makes the list. The Space or Rehab put on the best house nights in town, and for pure hedonists, Federation @ The Blank Canvas in Granary Wharf is a must.

Two Days On The Cheap

Stay – The Clock Hotel (0113 2930387 – £20 per night) on Rounday Road is well worth a look as is the Aintree Hotel on Cardigan Road (0113 275 8290 – £24 per night).
(Cost – £40 for two nights)

Shop – Hardly, but for a cool retro T-shirt try ReBop in the Corn Exchange, Positively 13 O'Clock, or try your luck at some of the many charity shops in Headingley.
(Cost £5 –but you'd better really like it)

Attractions – For free thrills, take a walk round Kirkstall Abbey, The City Art Gallery, The Royal Armouries or The Henry Moore Institute. A trip to Knaresborough to explore the dales will set you back a mere £5.30 (cheap day return), but you get all of that free fresh air into the bargain.
(Cost – £5.30)

Eat – You can do better than McDonalds, even on a tight budget. Viva Cuba is ace for bargainous tapas, and you'll get a good feed in any of Headingley's eateries for very few pounds. For central dining try Norman's or Tiger Tiger for decent lunchtime offers.
(Cost – £20)

Drink – Student favourites Walkabout, Bourbon and Qube are good for happy hours and drinks offers, as are The Oak and the Dry Dock if you can get your hands on a loyalty/yellow card. Bar Med in the financial district is good for cheap offers during the week, as is Mook.
(Cost – £20 should get you tipsy…)

Club – Entrance prices can be a bit steep, but try Creation before 10pm for free entry on week nights or £1 at weekends. HiFi will set you back between £4-£6, but with larger measures of spirits being served, you're bound to spend a bit less on booze.
(Cost – £9.70, all you have left)

Total £100

Days Out

Proper Yorkshire Slap & Tickle

When to go: Any day you fancy, pref sunny
Where to go:
Morning – Dig out your flat cap and head to the Henry Moore Institute to check out the work of one of Leeds' most famous inhabitants. To engage with local tradesfolk, get bartering at Kirkgate Market.

Lunch – Head to a traditional Yorkshire pub – Whitelocks or the Angel are good for solid pub grub. Both are central but still out of the way of the shops – perfect for pretending you're in the heart of Emmerdale Country.

Afternoon – Head to the Dales for a stroll in the countryside. A pint of bitter is a must – if there's a dog and an open fire, award yourself a bonus pint of Tetley's.

Evening – After all that fresh air you may be feeling a bit light-headed, so head to Joseph's Well for some local music. Talent is variable, but you just might see Yorkshire's answer to Bon Jovi. After sampling some more ale on offer, head home to watch a Heartbeat re-run... Smashing.

Extreme Sightseeing

When to go: Midweek – avoid the crowds
Where to go:
Morning – Start with a big breakfast at Citrus in Headingley. Have a wander down the high street, picking up some bedtime reading in Oxfam books or jewellery for the old lady in Azendi. As soon as The Original Oak opens, get in there and have a swift half in the beer garden.

Lunch – Head to town and browse (quickly) round the Henry Moore Institute, City Art Gallery and Craft Centre and Design Gallery. Nearby La Bonavita serves up quality antipasti – saving time deciding on what you fancy.

Afternoon – The Royal Armouries is a must, and all that armour should get you fired up. Head into town for a few frames of pool at The Elbow Room or have a sit down in Aire whilst looking over the canal. Finish off with a browse round Briggate's shops.

Evening – A burger at the Hard Rock should keep the fatigue at bay, then stimulate your mind at the West Yorkshire Playhouse. Round off the night with a few jars at The Northern Light – open 'til 2am during the week if you think you can handle it.

Ford**Fiesta**

Use your car for what it was designed for

Fiesta v. The Brontës

You can take the easy route. Or you can make like a Fiesta, rip up the rule book and have some fun. Listen to your Fiesta and get the both of you stuck into the rough and ready way of the bleak moors to Haworth. Your Fiesta dreams of showing you what it's made of.

Morning

Point your Fiesta in the direction of Otley, bumbling along on the slightly tedious A660. Hang a left there onto the B6451 – your Fiesta'll get a bit more excited as the road hots up. Left at Summer Bridge and up to Pateley Bridge. Zip across the village and on to the wicked back lanes towards Lofthouse, and then on to Leighton and Masham.

Lunch

After all that you'll be wanting some form of nourishment. Park your Fiesta up for a sec and quickly nip into Masham for a Theakston shandy and lunch at The Kings Head Hotel. Don't dally for too long – you promised your Fiesta some fun, remember?

Afternoon

Now, get onto the A6108 and take a left at Middleham on to some properly wild back lanes through the Dales. Take a left at Kettlewell onto the B6160 and follow the road all the way down to Grassington, hanging a right onto the B6265 to Skipton.

After Skipton, back lane it all the way from Glusburn over Keighley Moor through Brontë country via Goose Eye before hitting the bottom of Haworth High Street. Let your Fiesta show off up the hill, smug in the knowledge that you're not a Victorian woman in a big old dress struggling up all those cobbles with a basket of bread.

Itchy info

Kings Head Hotel, Market Place, Masham (01765) 685295

Brontë Parsonage Museum, Haworth (01535) 642323. £4.80/£3.50 – opening times vary please call.

restaurants

www.itchyleeds.co.uk

highlights

- **Contemporary chic at The Calls Grill**
- **Lightning fast udon at Fuji Hiro**
- **Mojitios and tapas at Viva Cuba**

lowlights

- **Pissed-up pubbers at Tariqs**
- **The mission to get to Maxis**
- **UK/US relations turned sour at Frankie & Benny's**

American

TGI Fridays
Wellington Street (0113) 242 8103

Right on the end of town and that's exactly where it should stay. The food ain't bad (big portions of hearty Americana) but the geeky outfits, robotic waiters and squealing school kids are enough to drive a person to homicide. Which wouldn't necessarily be a bad thing.

Mon-Sat 12pm-11pm, Sun 12pm-10.30pm
Chicken wings £7.45 House wine: £9.75

Frankie and Benny's
Cardigan Fields, Kirkstall (0113) 203 8888

About as Italian as a mug of Tetley's. It may well be the only Italian American gaff in Leeds, but come on, if you set up a Hawaiian restaurant you'd have to do more than don a grass skirt. Italian scrawlings on the walls, lessons in the toilets and a bumper pack of Grecian 2000 do not a Little Italy make. The only phrase you need to know here is 'where's the door?'

Sun-Thu 12pm-10.30pm, Fri-Sat till 11pm
Penne pasta pesto & chicken £7.35
House wine: £8.95

Hard Rock Café
The Cube, Albion Street (0113) 200 1310

Dine in the presence of greatness (or at least their clothes) at Hard Rock while reminiscing about some of the (soft) rock greats. Food is burger oriented, though there are some salads for more slender patrons. Get stuck into the cocktail menu and leave with The Summer of '69 ringing in your ears and a spring in your step. Rock on dude.

Mon-Fri 12pm-11pm,
Sat-Sun 11am-12am/1am
Jumbo combo £13.95 House wine: £11.25

recommended

Fancy food

Thai Edge
Livebait
Pool Court at 42
Teppenyaki
The Calls Grill
Ferret Hall Bistro
Harvey Nichols 4th Floor

English

Babylon
10 York Place (0113) 234 3344

Flash bar and restaurant on York Place, it's always been popular during the week with suits from the surrounding offices, but is now busier at the weekend thanks to all the bars springing up around the Financial District. The downstairs restaurant serves a strong range of modern British and Mediterranean dishes with an express lunchtime menu that's handy for clock watchers. It's renowned for its impressive surroundings and lavish evening menu, though the lack of windows in the restaurant can make you feel like you're dining in a very upmarket prison. Still, with a swish cocktail bar upstairs and a cool games room hidden in the back, you probably wouldn't mind being sent down for an 18 month stretch in here.
Mon-Wed 11am-11pm,
Tue-Sat 11am-12.30am
T-Bone steak £18 House wine: £9.95

Browns
The Headrow (0113) 243 9353

Browns serve Brit-with-a-twist style food in tropical-colonial surroundings, which like most of the colonies could do with a lick of paint as it's starting to feel a bit run down. They have more covers than any other restaurant in Leeds, and as such get's busy with large groups of office parties who are usually too pissed to care about the very average food. If you're considering a romantic meal for two, you'd be well advised dining somewhere a tad more intimate – like a runway.
Mon-Sat 11am-11pm, Sun 12pm-12.30am
Steak pie £7.95 House wine: £10.75

www.itchycity.co.uk

The Calls Grill
38 The Calls (0113) 245 3870

THE CALLS GRILL
LEEDS

RESTAURANT
MON-SAT 5.30PM-10.30PM

RECLAIM BAR
MON-WED 12PM-11PM
THUR-SAT 12PM-1AM
SUN 12PM-10.30PM

38 THE CALLS, LEEDS LS2 7EW
TELEPHONE: 0113 245 3870

Comfortably regarded as one of the best restaurants in Leeds, this multi award-winning family-owned restaurant on The Calls has been serving up top-notch steaks, seafood, meat and vegetarian dishes for the last five years. Its riverside location and fine food make it a top restaurant for romantic meals and more than justify the price, whilst the early bird offer of £10 for a main with either starter or dessert makes it accessible to everyone. You can also carry on drinking after dinner at the rather fabulous Reclaim bar downstairs.
Mon-Sat 5.30pm-10.30pm
Sirloin steak from £12.95
House wine: £10.95

Ferret Hall Bistro
2 The Parade (0113) 275 8613
The Ferret is everything a restaurant should be, a friendly husband and wife team have run it for years, and they've created an eatery with a surprisingly warm and relaxed atmosphere. The food is as accomplished as any in the city with a modern British menu revolving around meats, poultry and game, plus the wine list is, like any good wine list, very long. You must pay it a visit.
Mon-Sun 6pm-10pm
Kleftico of lamb £13.50
House wine: £10.95

Harvey Nichols 4th Floor
107 Briggate (0113) 204 8000
Very impressive restaurant serving scrummy food at not so nice prices ensuring there's no risk of mingling with peasants. If you can blag your boyfriend's credit card you'll find the modern Brit dishes are divine and the desserts to die for. Just be prepared when the gorgeous waiter brings over a portion so small it'd barely knock dead an ant.
Mon-Wed 10am-6pm, Thu 10am-10pm,
Sat 9am-10pm, Sun 12pm-5pm
Rib-eye steak £12 House wine: £13.50

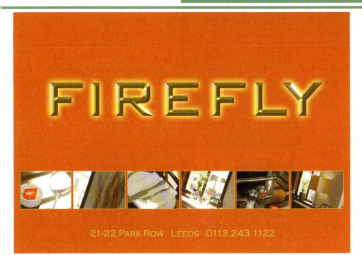

FIREFLY

21-22 PARK ROW LEEDS 0113 243 1122

Firefly
21 Park Row (0113) 243 1122

Firefly offers fine dining in the financial district providing a boost to the area's restaurant scene that has sent the city's cluster of accountants and solicitors scrambling for their company credit cards. Firefly focuses on putting innovative twists on well-known dishes with some very good a la carte options of seafood, poultry and game, and tasty specials supported by a strong wine list. The adjacent bar offers a great opportunity to stay for plenty of drinks after your meal, and the staff are friendly too. Really friendly. They'd probably even phone in plausible excuses on your behalf when you can't return to the office for the rest of the afternoon.

A la carte: Mon-Sat 12pm-11pm, Sun 12pm-10.30pm
Fixed priced menu: 2 courses for £10, 3 courses for £12.95 (Mon-Thu 12pm-11pm, Fri-Sat 12pm-7pm)
Brunch menu: Sun 12pm-6pm

Leodis

Sovereign Street (0113) 242 1010

One of Leeds' firm favourites (it's been around since 1992), many places try (and fail) to compete with its cosmopolitan menu. It also manages to stay on the right side of up-its-own-arse making it a fine choice for special occasions.

Mon-Fri 12pm-2pm & 6pm-10pm,
Sat 6pm-10pm
Roast beef £11.50 House wine: £13.95

No 3 York Place

3 York Place (0113) 245 9922

Simon Gueller has moved on to greener pastures and taken his name with him. Now renamed No 3 York Place, you'll find this place in the heart of the financial quarter serving up high quality French and British food. You'll have to hammer the expense account for a decent feed, but they say you get what you pay for, and here they're kind of right.

Mon-Fri 12pm-2pm & 6.30pm-10.30pm,
Sat 6.30pm-10pm
Poached saddle of rabbit £14.95
House wine: £15.50

Northern Light

Cross York Street (0113) 243 6446

The trains might not be up to much but the link between London and Leeds is as strong as ever with this impressive display of food, drink and architecture. Northern Light is the sister bar to Shoreditch's E1 The Light (lauded by the likes of Alexander McQueen) and is utterly impressive. Sink into its classy environs and tuck into some spot on locally sourced organic/modern British fare: lunchtime deli skewer wraps are excellent. You'll instantly feel like the pop star you might have been if you hadn't been born to a pair of layabout wasters from Meanwood. Drown your sorrows in the swanky bar/club afterwards – it's open 'til 2am.

Mon-Sat 12pm-10.30pm (restaurant)
Mon-Thu 12pm-12am, Fri-Sat 12pm-2am (bar)
Mon-Sat 9pm-2am (club in term-time),
Thu-Sat 9pm-2am (club out of term time)
2 courses for £10, 3 for £13
Smoked Whitby haddock £10
House wine: £9.50

Pool Court at 42
44 The Calls (0113) 244 4242

Leeds' highest rated restaurant and the proud owner of a Michelin star (the only venue in Leeds to have one), it's rightfully located in the trendy Calls area of the city as part of stylish hotel 42 The Calls. It's small (seating only 35) and expensive, but should make any first date a sure thing

Mon-Thu 12pm-2pm & 7pm-10pm,
Fri 7pm-10.30pm, Sat 7pm-11.30pm
Pool Court's fillet of Scottish beef
wellington £18.75 House wine: £13

The Reliance
76 North Street (0113) 295 6060

This bistro/bar deserves a mention – the effort they haven't made with the furniture is more than made up for with a gallant effort with the food. Come here for a classy take on pub grub, hangover defying breakfasts and hearty Sunday roasts. Takes forever to get served on a Sunday but it's worth it.

Mon-Sat 12pm-11pm, Sun 12pm-10.30pm
Food: Sun 12pm-4pm & 6pm-10pm, Mon-
Sat 12pm-5pm & 6pm-10.30pm
Sunday brunch £5-£7.50 House wine: £12

French

Café Rouge
Waterloo House, Crown Street
(0113) 245 1551

About as authentically French as a cheese 'n' pickle sandwich, you get exactly what you came for at Café Rouge. Franglais cuisine – fries, salads, moules, baguettes – a congregation of buggy-wielding stay-at-home moms and a redeemingly nice location. Leave your GSCE French babblings at the door though, the staff aren't French and don't even bother to pretend to be, which is disappointing.

Mon-Fri 11pm-10pm, Sat-Sun 10am-10pm
Sirloin steak £11 House wine: £9.95

La Grillade
27 Wellington Street (0113) 245 8856

Cracking French eaterie in the basement of the swanky new apartment complex that was The Wellesley hotel. It's a bit grittier than its nearby rivals, which is actually a good thing as you feel like you've conspiratorially stumbled across a hidden treasure. The food is very good and well priced with noveau cuisine bashingly large portions, and the absence of any windows justifies at least three bottles of wine with lunch. Plus there's a ginger bespectacled waiter who you'd swear is called Nigel and comes from Stoke, but is actually French.

Mon-Fri 12pm-2.30pm & 7pm-10.30pm,
Sat 7pm-11pm
Cut de boeuf en chateau brianne for two
£24 House wine: £11.90

Sous Le Nez En Ville
Quebec Street (0113) 244 0108

A free itchy guide to anywhere you want to anyone who can email us the correct translation of the name. Smelly town is popular with the more mature, well-heeled clientele who frequent the multitude of surrounding offices. The menu is diverse and delicious, and the wine list enormous. The waiters are also friendly enough, steering away from the arrogant stereotype, and there's also a huge photo on the wall of a team of award-winning chefs that's reminiscent of a chubby French World Cup squad – perhaps they'd have had a more fruitful time in Japan than Zidane and his buddies too, eh?

Mon-Fri 12pm-2.30pm & 6pm-10pm,
Sat 12pm-2.30pm & 6pm-11pm
Fillet steak £17.50 House wine: £10.95

Mon - Thur
12pm-5pm

nachos,
bocadillos &
jacket potatoes
all 2-4-1
with valid
student ID

opening hours
Mon - Fri
12pm-11pm

Sat
12pm-12am
Sun
12pm-10.30pm

CUBAN HEELS

0113 234 6115
behind corn
exchange

recommended 👍

Cheap Eats

brb All day Tue & Thu evenings
(2-4-1 pizzas)
Tiger Tiger Mon-Fri 12pm-5pm
(lunch menu £3)
Bar Med All the time
(4 tapas & bottle of wine £9.95)
Shabab Mon-Fri 11.45am-2.15pm &
Mon-Sat 6.30pm-9.30pm (eat as much as
you like buffet £7.99 Mon-Thu, £8.99
Fri-Sat)
The Box Mon-Fri 12pm-6pm (£3.50 meal
deal pizzas, burgers, nachos etc)
Café Rouge Mon-Fri 12pm-5pm (£7.95 2
course menu)
Caffe Uno Wed-Sat 12pm-10pm (starter,
main course & bottle of wine £15)

Italian

Bibis
Minerva House, Greek Street
(0113) 243 0905

Wins few points for its white wicker, glass and mirrored décor (too OTT on-the-cheap glitz for anyone who isn't a footballer) but the scran is good, so we'll probably let them off. Bibis is surprisingly popular in foodie circles and its business district location means it's always full of expense accounts being well exercised. You'll find it rammed at weekends and one of the few places in town that gets busy on Sunday evenings.

Mon-Fri 12pm-2.15pm & 6pm-11.15pm,
Sat 5.30pm-11.15pm, Sun 6pm-10.30pm
Cappelletti al prosciutto £7.25
House wine: £13.25

Brio
Great George Street (0113) 246 5225
Tucked away behind the town hall and well worth seeking out. The evening menu changes from Italian pizzas and ciabattas to offer up some anglo-French style. Classy and totally approachable.
Mon-Fri 12pm-2.30pm & 6pm-10.30pm,
Sat 6pm-10pm
Steak with garlic & mushroom sauce £16
House wine: £10

Da Mario's
105 The Headrow (0113) 246 0390
Da Mario's is in many ways the ideal first date restaurant: homely, full of character, not very expensive, and most importantly not very good food – you'll have your date racing home to bed in a taxi in next to no time – my God you're good.
Mon-Fri 12pm-2pm & 5pm-10.30pm,
Sat 12pm-10.30pm, Sun 5pm-10pm
Spaghetti marinara £6.45
House wine: £9.95

Dino's
1 Bishopgate Street (0113) 231 4241
The Majestyk of the restaurant scene, it's big, it's near the station, everyone's been here at some point, and you can't help but enjoy yourself. It's great when you're tipsy, though-when sober you'll notice that the food is covered in more olive oil than Popeye's inside leg, still that shouldn't stop you from rocking up at all hours and drinking them out of cheap white wine.
Mon-Sat 12pm-2pm & 6pm-11pm,
Sun 5.30pm-11pm
Petto di pollo alexandra £10.75
House wine: £10.75

Est Est Est
31-33 East Parade (0113) 246 0669
151 Otley Road (0113) 267 2100
A homage to 80s minimalism, and an interesting twist on Pizza Express's formula of reasonably-priced, ok food, served in nice surroundings. The East Parade venue is popular with suits too tight to give the expense account a proper thrashing and hen nights at the start of their dildo-weilding adventures. The Otley Road branch is popular with friends of the waiters, who sit at the bar asking their mate why it's always so quiet. 'Because we're miles from anywhere' he replies, 'but we sometimes get a student party in, or a few couples on a first date. It's easier to go to Pizza Express'.
Mon-Sun 12pm-11pm
Calzone pizza £7.45 House wine: £10.95

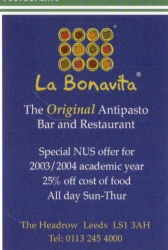

La Bonavita ®

The *Original* Antipasto Bar and Restaurant

Special NUS offer for 2003/2004 academic year 25% off cost of food All day Sun-Thur

The Headrow Leeds LS1 3AH
Tel: 0113 245 4000

La Bonavita
The Headrow (0113) 245 4000

Sounds Italian and serves Italian food, wine and beer though it's run by Brits who've decided that the UK needs a bit of culture in its otherwise bland, culinary existence. Its antipasto dishes (the same idea as Spanish tapas) are tasty and well priced, and also partly targeted at vegans and veggies (a true rarity). Top it off with one of the best outside seating areas in Leeds, some of the friendliest and most efficient service around and you're on to an absolute winner. More of an informal eaterie than posh a la carte affair – even folks on their lonesome will feel right at home. Result.

Mon-Wed 11am-10pm,
Thu-Sat 11am-11pm, Sun 12pm-8pm
Polpette alla romana £3.95
House wine: £9.95

Pietro
70 Otley Road (0113) 274 4262

This is one of those 'little place I know' deals offering up top-notch, proper Italian food, friendly service, a cosy atmosphere and prices that are nowhere near worthy of the food. For the first time ever what we mean by this is that they're probably too cheap. Slip them an extra tenner on your way out and offer them your first born child to train up as a master. Bloody fantastic.

Mon closed, Tue-Thu 6pm-10.30pm,
Fri-Sat 6pm-11pm, Sun 5pm-10pm
Chicken athena £7.95 House wine: £8.95

Pizza Express
Crown Street (0113) 244 5858

'Fiorentina and the dough balls for me, and my mate'll have a Sloppy Guiseppe…and no we don't need to look at the menu.'

Sun-Wed 10am-11pm,
Thu-Sat 10am-11.30pm
Polla astra £7.95 House wine: £10.95

Salvos
115 Otley Road (0113) 275 5017

Extremely popular Headingley Italian, it's been here for years, built up a loyal customer base and is nearly always rammed. The food's very good but you spend the evening crushed up closely with your fellow diners, firstly waiting for a table in the tiny bar (you can't book) and then sat practically on each others laps as the tables are so close together. You can't help longing to dine somewhere more spacious, like a submarine. Best time to go is for the two courses for a fiver lunchtime extravaganza.

Mon-Sat 12pm-2pm, Mon-Thu 6pm-10.45pm, Fri-Sat 5.30pm-11pm
Brasato d'agnello £12.75
House wine: £11.50

Greek

Dimitri's
20 Dock Street (0113) 246 0339

As if living next to the canal in a flash and obscenely expensive apartment in the swankiest area of town wasn't enough, those folks who inhabit The Calls get Dimitri's too. One of the nicest, friendliest restaurants in town, it serves up tasty Greek/Mediterranean dishes including an impressive range of tapas and meze at a pretty decent prices, sometimes to the sound of a visiting band. The atmosphere and décor will raise your spirits when you realise you can't afford a trendy riverside pad. It's better to be happy than rich.

Mon-Sun 11am-12am
Kleftico £12.65 House wine: £10.95

Indian

Akbars
Eastgate (0113) 245 6566

Popular new boy on Eastgate that serves up pretty good food in flash surroundings. The naan breads are the stuff of legend and by rights should be a meal in themselves, spiked on a huge skewer like a trophy to your manly appetite. They cram in as many tables as possible and with the large number of staff if can feel very claustrophobic. Also it's non-smoking which may not help your frayed nerves, but you should be calmed by the fact that it's very cheap - it's priced like a student curry house, yet the food is very good – what a happy bundle of contradictions it is.

Sun-Thu 5pm-12am, Fri-Sat 5pm-12.30am
Karahi chicken £4.95 House wine: £6.95

Darbar
16 Kirkgate (0113) 246 0381

Feeling a little down? Well, forget that Lean Cuisine waiting for you at home and let the exotic cuisine of Darbar warm your cockles. Even though it resembles an Indian palace and serves up some of the best curry in the city, the best thing about this place is the exotic fruit basket at the end. For anyone who grew up impoverished/during a world war it's like the education in fruit they never had. And for those ladies who feel like they've been left on the shelf, the cheeky waiter with the chocolates will have you discovering your inner beauty once more.
Mon-Sat 6pm-11.30pm
Lamb balti £10.95 House wine: £9.95

Elephant Curry Café
16 Merrion Street (0113) 243 9352

One of the few places in town where you can get a late night curry at the weekend, and hence everyone in here is usually worse for wear after too much European fighting juice. The staff are friendly and very patient with their pissed-up punters, and if you tell them it's your birthday they'll even give you free liqueurs – like you'll really need another drink – which isn't such a bad idea as the food isn't very good. There are lots of better Indian restaurants around; nonetheless, if you're stuck in town titted and twatted, and you fancy a ruby, then it's all aboard the Elephant.. "Oi, oi!"
Mon-Thu 5.30pm-11.30pm,
Fri-Sat 5.30pm-3.30am
Chicken bhuna £5 House wine: £8.95

Shabab
2 Eastgate (0113) 246 8988

Everything's just as it should be here – Marharaja palace style décor, waiters with flair and fantastic, firey Indian delights. Shabab is Leeds' oldest Indian restaurant offering all-you-can-eat lunchtime buffets and impressive a la carte to a crowd that

stop short of the lager fuelled boisterousness of your usual late night crowd. It can offer an intimate candlelit dining experience that's good for romantic couples, whilst also catering for large groups making it a strong choice for birthday parties and hen nights. All the classics are there on the menu along with some accomplished house specialities – go for these; they're unique, very tasty and much more interesting. Its city centre location also makes it very handy for post-meal partying in the city.
Mon-Sun 11.30am-2.30pm &
6pm-11.45pm
Neahari £7.50 House wine: £10.90

Think we're wrong? Go to www.itchycity.co.uk

GreatPeopletoDineWith

Eat as much as you like buffets or a la
carte choice at the oldest established
Indian restaurant in Leeds.

Lunch: Mon-Fri 11.45 - 2.15pm
Evening: Everyday 6pm - 11.45pm
Closed Christmas Day and New Years Day

2 Eastgate, Leeds, LS2 7JL
Tel: 0113 246 8988

1099 Thornton Road, Bradford BD8 0PA
01274 815 760

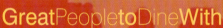

Email: info@shababrestaurants.co.uk

www.shababrestaurants.co.uk

Spice 4 U

8b-10b Market Street (0113) 243 3737
36 North St, Wetherby (01937) 583694
41 Hungate, Pickering (01751) 473334

With restaurants in Leeds, Wetherby and Pickering in just three years, this Yorkshire mini chain is set to take over the world. And when they do, we certainly won't want for any fantastically prepared Indian and Bangladeshi cuisine. You'll find everything you could ask for from an Indian restaurant here with excellent balti and tandoori dishes and plenty of spicy specials served up in fantastically modern and colourful surroundings. It's also a known hangout of the Leeds stars and even Kevin Keegan, so it's clearly a good place to enjoy yourself whilst waiting for the transfer window to open.
Leeds: 12pm-12am; Pickering: 6pm-12am
Wetherby: 5pm-12am (all open daily)
Bindiya chicken £7.50 House wine: £8.50

Tariq's

12-16 St Michael's Road (0113) 275 1881
Most visitors to this place have little memory in the morning and it's not because of the rapturous joy of the food. To be fair it ain't bad (it's actually rather tasty) but the clientele are definitely of the scarily-drunk-but think-they're-not ilk. Cue boys in DJs shout-

ing 'I am Mumra' and girls in tight tops flashing their tits. There is a takeaway next door which frankly they should probably frequent instead.

Mon-Thu 5pm-1am, Fri-Sat 5pm-3am,
Sun 5pm-12am
Chicken tikka masala £5
House wine: £6.50

Chinese

28 28 Chinese Buffet Menu
Gower Street (0113) 242 6174

Join hordes of regulars to gorge yourself on Chinese all-you-can-eat. Raise your thumbs aloft to the sweet and sour and dare your date to try that random looking dark meat on the end. The emphasis is firmly on quantity not quality, but judging by the clientele that's exactly what they're after.

Tue-Sun 12pm-3pm,
Tue-Sun 5.30pm-11pm, Sun 6pm-9pm
Buffet £6 (£10 in the evening)
House wine: £9.20

Canton Flavour
The Headrow (0113) 246 8860

Dinner time restaurant for lardy suited types seeking a grease-lined feed. They do great lunch time deals too – spot on if you're a regular down the gym, death to your abs if it's straight back to the car and a life of gluttony for you. Leeds isn't great for oriental cuisine, but Canton Flavour makes a decent bid at dragging us into the cultural mix. It's a bit dingy inside - good if last week's rampage of fags and tequila is starting to show under your eyes.

Mon-Sat 11.30am-11pm, Sun 12pm-11pm
Red chicken curry £6.50 House wine: £8.95

Lucky Dragon
Lady Lane (0113) 245 0520

Pile 'em high and sell 'em cheap, that's what we say. And Lucky Dragon says it too, although probably in more of a Chinese accent. Confucius say, 'man with prawn cracker mountain make good lover'. Umm anyway, Lucky Dragon has some reasonable offers: from a stuff-your-fat-face buffet to cheap meal deals. You'll find it located in the comically sparse China 'town' (one restaurant, two shops, a travel agent, and a Lebanese café). Try the Sunday buffet as an alternative to your mum's burnt carrots.

Mon-Sun 12pm-12am
Cantonese steak £10 House wine: £11.50

Maxi's
6 Bingley Street (0113) 244 0552

Maxi's even has its own arch for authenticity. Head for this massive celebration of all things Chinese and dare yourself to step into the territory beyond chicken with cashew nuts. You'll need a small orienteering kit to find the place – it's kind of behind the casino and bathroom place on the road into town from Kirkstall. Pack yourself off with some Kendal mint cake and an open mind, and sample some of the finest food in Leeds.

Mon-Sun 12pm-12am
King prawns £9.70 House wine: £9.90

Japanese

56 Oriental Restaurant
56 Wellington Street (0113) 245 0380

So minimal you'll feel like you need to tidy up after yourself and polish the door handle on the way out (you can't even smoke in the main upstairs bit), this place is finely tuned to the needs of the surrounding hotshot financial types. The service has military precision and the food is a fabulous mix of regional noodle-type dishes.

Mon-Fri 12pm-2.30pm & 5pm-11pm,
Sat 12pm-2.30pm & 6pm-11pm, Sun
12pm-2.30pm & 6pm-10.30pm
Meegoreng £7.95 House wine: £9.95

Fuji Hiro
45 Wade Lane (0113) 243 9184

Fuji Hiro is a fantastic little noodle bar around the back of the Merrion Centre. The idea is to provide a kind of fast food environment, but without the slash-your-wrists-style depressive tendencies of the nearby McDonald's. Smiling staff will rush you bowls of ramen, fried squid and udon quicker than you can say 'konnichiwa'. Closely set formica tables mean you'll be forced to show your embarrassing incompetence with chopsticks to strangers, but that's the price you pay for fast living. It's cheap too.

Sun-Fri 12pm-10pm, Fri-Sat 12pm-11pm
Yaki soba £5.75 Beer £2.50

Little Tokyo
24 Central Road (0113) 243 9090

If you want to get all culturally superior about it all, Little Tokyo is actually run and staffed by people from Japan – something of a rarity in Leeds. There's a great selection of sushi and they offer half versions, and beginner sushi (for wusses who get freaked by raw fish) at bargainous prices. Add to this well-presented bento and a new found affiliation with Teppanyaki and all well's in this part of town.

Mon-Thu 11.30am-10pm, Fri-Sat till 11pm
Sashimi bento £6.95 House wine: £9.50

Shogun Teppan-Yaki
Granary Wharf (0113) 245 1856

Quite possibly the only reason anyone ever descends into the depths of Granary Wharf of an evening. Give it a try and find that, to your surprise, you'll not be greeted by a gang of vampires ready to suck your mortal blood but a rather flash Japanese restaurant that specialises in flames. Chefs throw food around over the kind of fire normally associated with a ten-year stretch for arson whilst the punters try to conceal their terror. We assure you it's worth the fear.

Mon-Sun 12pm-2pm & 6pm-10.30pm
House special £26 House wine: £9.50

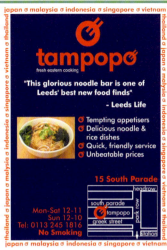

japan σ malaysia σ indonesia σ singapore σ vietnam

tampopo
fresh eastern cooking

"This glorious noodle bar is one of Leeds' best new food finds"

- Leeds Life

- σ Tempting appetisers
- σ Delicious noodle & rice dishes
- σ Quick, friendly service
- σ Unbeatable prices

15 South Parade

Mon-Sat 12-11
Sun 12-10
Tel: 0113 245 1816
No Smoking

japan σ malaysia σ indonesia σ singapore σ vietnam

ish and a Godsend for the health conscious. If you're not already an out an out fan then give this place a go as soon as you can.
Mon-Sat 12pm-11pm, Sun 12pm-2.30pm
Chicken with chilli & lemongrass £7.25
House wine: £10.95

Teppanyaki
Belgrave Hall, Belgrave Street (0113) 245 3345

Another Japanese teppanyaki restaurant for the legions of fans of the genre – tasty, fresh fish, meat and vegetable dishes seared to perfection while you wait. This flame throwing spectacular is nearer the city centre and totally innovative. Makes a fine change from microwave lasagne.
Mon-Fri 12pm-2pm, Mon-Sat 6pm-11pm
Yakitori £9.50 House wine: £10.50

Organic

Tampopo
15 South Parade (0113) 245 1816

A Leeds institution these days – Tampopo offers fabulous noodle and rice dishes in a slick Japanese canteen-style restaurant. It's popular with local business types who appreciate the military efficiency of the service, as well as hip young things chilling out with some tasty food. It's delicious, styl-

The Millrace
2 Commercial Road (0113) 275 7555

Drive past the Warner Village and you might think you've driven into the Yorkshire equivalent of a Midwestern trailer park. Look harder though because you haven't. The Millrace serves up tasty organic fodder (all ingredients are certified by the Soil Association or UK Farmers and Growers Association) and even has a smoking lounge upstairs for after dinner drinks. Flash as you like and before you ask, no organic does not mean vegetarian. Tuck in to a guilt-free hunk of flesh.
Tue-Sat 5.30pm-11pm
Sunday lunch served from 12pm
Sunday roast £10.95 (3 courses)
House wine: £10.95

Mexican Restaurant
www.cactuslounge.com

St Peters Square Leeds
0113 243 6553

from Cactus Lounge.
Mon-Fri 12pm-2.30pm,
Mon-Wed 5pm-9.30pm, Thu-Sat 5pm-late
Lunchtime special: 2 courses for £5.45
Pre-theatre deal: Mon-Sat 5pm-7pm, 2
course & glass wine/beer £9.95
Chicken fajitas £11.95 House wine: £9.95

Cactus Lounge
St Peter's Building, St Peter's Square
(0113) 243 6553
Check out Cactus Lounge and chuck yourself head on into its slick and stylish interior,
upbeat buzz and fantastic modern Mexican
food. Tuck into bargain lunchtime food with
Leeds College of Music and West Yorkshire
Playhouse types (the restaurant's alongside
both in the city's mini cultural centre) or get
down to some fine tequila-fuelled banter
with a group of your mates – the venue
caters very well for large groups and is a top
choice for birthdays or hen/stag dos. It's also
handily close to The Wardrobe for after
hours action, plus you get discounted entry
to their club if you show your meal receipt

Caliente Café
53 Otley Road (0113) 274 9841
"The best Tex-Mex this side of the Rio
Grande (and possibly even the other)" so
proclaims Kinky 'the kinkster' Freidman, and
I for one am not going to argue with a man
called Kinky. It's long been a Headingley staple offering up not only the best Mexican
but the best food in studentville. They've

CALIENTE CAFÉ™

AND

MEXICAFE®™ NIGHTS

GOURMET SOUTHWEST & TEX MEX
30 YEARS OF QUALITY
53 OTLEY ROAD LEEDS LS6 3AB
TEL: 0113 274 9841
© KP PROPERTY   ART, DESIGN, SIGNAGE & FASCIA
ALL RIGHTS RESERVED © 2003

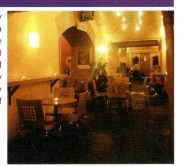

introduced a new menu for Sunday, Monday and Tuesday evenings which offers up a selection of the usual; as well as a few more unusual options (the Huevos Ranchos rock) and every dish is £7 or less. The food will never dissapoint, the decor's vaguely Mexican and the staff are friendly. The only criticism is they don't take plastic, but if Kinky can pay in cash so can you, amigo.
Mon-Tue closed, Wed-Sun 6.30pm-10.30pm
Chicken enchilada £7.95 House wine: £7.95

Cuban Heels

28-30 Assembly Street (0113) 234 6115
The owner of Cuban Heels very cannily spotted the Mexican trend of the last decade, and was the first to open up a restaurant/bar in railway arches near trendy Call Lane. It's still going strong now, specialising in large portions of Cuban, Cajun and Mexican dishes, and you're equally welcome to just rock up for beers and slammers in the bar. Neck some tequila in here before stumbling next door to shake your ass in Fudge.
Mon-Thu 12pm-9.30pm,
Fri-Sat 12pm-11.30pm
Chicken fajitas £8.95 House wine: £8.95

Seafood

Livebait
The Calls (0113) 244 4144

Sea creatures galore – fresh, dead and ready for the eating (bring a tool kit if you're planning to tackle the platter). There's outside seating, a swanky but chilled vibe and slick exposed stone/glass décor. Staff know their stuff – they have GCSEs and everything.

Mon-Thu 12pm-3pm & 5.45pm-10.30pm,
Fri-Sat 12pm-3pm & 5.45pm-11pm,
Sun closed
Six Indian Ocean crevettes £9
House wine: £9.95

Spanish

La Tasca
Greek Street (0113) 244 2205

It's such a simple idea that it's surprising that no one thought of it before, but La Tasca's brand of cheering us up by recreating the Spanish tavernas from holidays past seems to work really well. It's popular with large groups and you don't have to book, hence everyone crams round a large table to enjoy all sorts of tapas. It really is a case of the more the merrier, as by ordering a multitude of dishes that are pretty reasonable, eventually it works out that what one person loathes, someone else will love. Everyone gets well fed and has a good time – as clear an expression of utopian socialism in dining as you could hope for.

Mon-Sun 12pm-11pm
Patatas bravas £2.95 House wine: £9.45

Thai

Sala Thai
13-17 Shaw Lane (0113) 278 8400

Looks very imposing from the outside, but for somewhere in far Headingley way outside of the city centre, it can afford the space to be a bit of a show off. Inside is equally decadent with waitresses dressed in Thai costume and a thoroughly impressive Thai menu.

Mon-Sat 6pm-10.30pm
Chicken in green curry £7.45
House wine: £8.50

Thai Edge
New Portland Place, 7 Calverley Street (0113) 243 6333

Expensive Thai restaurant overlooking Millennium Square, though if the view's included in the price, I'd be asking for a refund. Inside it's authentic and beautiful – orchids, waterfalls, waitresses in traditional dress and a minimalist feel make for a very serene dining experience. Leave the end of that fight about the cat food to the taxi on the way home.

Mon-Thu 12pm-2.30pm & 5.30pm-
11.30pm, Fri-Sat 12pm-2.30pm & 5.30pm-
12am, Sun 12pm-3pm & 6pm-11pm
Panang gai £7.90 House wine: £10

Other/Fusion

Art's

42 Call Lane (0113) 243 8243

Leeds' first café bar and probably still the best, Art's stands out as a true gem amongst a city of samey style bars and weird old men's boozers. A café by day providing chilled-out surroundings for a quick coffee and a gossip or lunchtime feed (the lunchtime plates for a fiver are fantastic, and a bargain), and a restaurant by night where you'll find a small but impressive menu ideal for wooing prospective partners or groveling to the parents. The real beauty of this place though is the local artwork exhibited on the wall that changes every month or so, get the inside track on the artists from the staff and then show off loudly about how cultured you are.

Mon-Sat 11am-11pm, Sun 11am-10.30pm
Lunch platters £5.50 House wine: £10.50

Brasserie 44

44 The Calls (0113) 234 3232

Brasserie 44 cannot be beaten in terms of contemporary cuisine. Their menus are at the cutting edge of restaurant chic without being overly trendy and prices are decidedly good value. The décor isn't quite to our tastes but then we still think chucking out your chintz is the height of hip.

Mon-Thu 12pm-2pm & 6pm-10.30pm, Fri 12pm-2pm & 6pm-11pm, Sat 6pm-11pm
Wontons £6.25 House wine: £16

Chino Latino

Park Plaza, City Square (0113) 380 4080

Chino Latino's second UK excursion offers a unique brand of Japanese and Far Eastern fusion cuisine combined with Latino styles. Situated in the Park Plaza hotel opposite the station, but open to non-residents too, Chino delivers a heady blend of culinary influences within cool dark minimalist surroundings. The restaurant combines flavours of Thai, Chinese and South East Asian food, with a Latino twist, with the menu including noodles, an array of sushi, and chicken thigh teriyaki alongside Argentinean beef, grilled meat and seafood, salads and fish. The stylish bar is also a good stop-off for drinks after work or before a night out, but you'll soon find your mind wandering to the blissful prospect of chowing down on the best of what two continents have offer.

Mon-Sat 12pm-3pm, Mon-Sat 6pm-10.30pm, Sun 6pm-10pm
Black cod tempura £14 House wine: £13

Citrus
13a North Lane (0113) 274 9002

The students of Headingley would probably up sticks and desert to Manchester if it wasn't for this place. Citrus serves up fry-ups, salads and fancy meat and fish dishes to its enthusiastic punters. There are some respectable staples of pizzas and pastas, but if you turn over the menu, you'll find some very accomplished and tasty main courses – I ate here for about 18 months before I noticed this. The waiting staff can be pretty slow, but they're obviously picked for their looks, so we forgive them. Good food, decent value: top marks.

Mon-Thu 9am-4.30pm & 5.30pm-10pm,
Fri 9am-4.30pm & 6pm-10pm,
Sat 10am-4pm & 6pm-10pm,
Sun 11am-4pm & 6pm-10pm
Steak with peppercorn sauce £9.75
House wine: £8.95

Tiger Tiger
The Light, The Headrow (0113) 236 6999

While the rest of Tiger Tiger ranges from the exotic to the more formal, the restaurant remains strictly minimalist. Food-wise though, they're more experimental in their tastes, combining classic dishes with modern influences. As well as offering an extensive a la carte menu, you can take advantage of their canapé and buffet menus or set party menu if it happens to be your turn to organise this year's office knees up. A smaller bar food menu is available for those fleeting lunches, available at half price during happy hour (daily 5pm-7.30pm).

Mon-Sun 12pm-2am
Pan roasted sea bass £12.95
House wine: £10.95

The Wardrobe
St Peter's Square (0113) 383 8800

The restaurant bit in The Wardrobe is pretty much part of the bar, though it does have a menu to rival most of the more upmarket eateries in the city. Serving up a contemporary menu in the evenings as well as light lunches and pre-theatre offers, here's one of the only places in the city where you can grab a bite to eat while listening to a quality band. It's not a huge restaurant area, but perfect for intimate meals with your other half, mates and prospective partners – they'll think you're dead cool and loaded with it – ha ha, the fools..

Mon-Sun 12pm-3pm & 5pm-10pm (tapas served all day)
Pre-theatre offer £12 two courses,
£14 three couses
Wardrobe fishcakes £8 House wine: £10

Viva Cuba
342 Kirkstall Road (0113) 275 0888

It's so easy to take a culturally dependent restaurant idea and hash it up completely (Frankie and Benny's take note) but Viva Cuba is one of the success stories. Tasty tapas that please the pocket, a friendly and intimate atmosphere and authentic Cuban knick-knacks (not just the obligatory Che

'THE MEALS ARE EXCELLENT ... LEEDS CAFE SOCIETY AT ITS BEST'
THE TIMES

'EXCELLENT FOOD AND GOOD VALUE IN A WARM, RELAXED AMBIENCE'
YORKSHIRE EVENING POST

arts
café bar restaurant
modern european and english cuisine

EARLY BIRD MENU MONDAY – THURSDAY 5–7PM   DAILY SPECIALS   LUNCH PLATES   EXTENSIVE WINE LIST
open monday – sunday 11am – 11pm
42 call lane leeds LS1 6DT   T: 0113 243 8243   www.artscafebar.co.uk

Guevara wallpaper). It's not the biggest restaurant in the world which means queueing at the bar at weekends is a must, but with the Havana rum flowing freely, the bar really is the best place to be.

Mon-Sat 6pm-11pm, Sun 6pm-10.30pm
Cod cakes £3.25
House wine: £10

Vegetarian

Hansa Gujirati
74 North Street (0113) 244 4408

If there ever was a restaurant to persuade you to down tools on that lump of cow and default to a world of vegetables and rights for chickens, then this place is surely it. The veggie Indian fare they serve here is second to none, properly spicy and 110% worth a visit. On top of that the place is cosy, good value, and has at least ten menu items you'll never even have heard of. Blinding and not in an eye way.

Mon-Sun 6pm-10.30pm
Bhagat muthiya £5.95 House wine: £11

bars

www.itchyleeds.co.uk

highlights

- Guest continental lagers at North Bar
- Pot holing in Oslo
- Flaring contests at Mixing Tin
- Hen parties, complete with boob tubes and bunny ears

lowlights

- Chilli vodka fracas at Revolution
- Getting lost on the way to Sutra

Exchange Quarter

brb
37 Call Lane (0113) 243 0315
Any bar on Call Lane is bound to be a hit with the punters at the weekend and brb is no exception. Location aside, it has made an effort to be a bit different, with chandeliers, a chill-out style room that looks like somebody's lounge and an upstairs club area perfect for showing off your Justin Timberlake moves. Pizza deals and drinks offers mid-week keep the masses flooding in, or at least those brave enough to get past the power happy bouncers who ask pointless questions at the door. Give it a rest lads.
Sun-Thu 12pm-12am, Fri 12pm-1am,
Sat 12pm-2am
Chilli chicken pizza £6.95 House wine: £10

Café Inseine
13 Duncan Street (0113) 242 2436
Café Inseine would receive far, far less custom if it wasn't situated so damn conveniently opposite HiFi. Some mad architect-type has chosen to fill the entire seating area with one long bar. Unless you've arrived at 7pm and grabbed one of the five (count 'em) available seats, you're doomed to standing and shouting at your mates over banging house. Good vantage point for the club queues, though. Watch and wait…
Mon-Thu 12pm-11pm, Fri-Sat 12pm-1am,

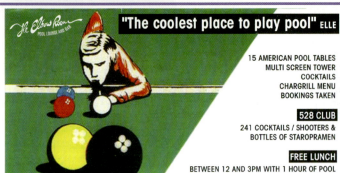

"The coolest place to play pool" ELLE

15 AMERICAN POOL TABLES
MULTI SCREEN TOWER
COCKTAILS
CHARGRILL MENU
BOOKINGS TAKEN

528 CLUB
241 COCKTAILS / SHOOTERS &
BOTTLES OF STAROPRAMEN

FREE LUNCH
BETWEEN 12 AND 3PM WITH 1 HOUR OF POOL

SUGARBEAT CLUB
EVERY SATURDAY
GUESTS INCLUDE: SOULWAX, CA$H MONEY, DOVES
KRAFTYKUTS, APHRODITE & MANY MORE

OPEN 7 DAYS A WEEK TILL LATE

THE ELBOW ROOM
64 CALL LANE, LEEDS LS1
0113 245 7011
leeds@theelbowroom.co.uk
www.theelbowroom.co.uk

The Elbow Room
34 Call Lane (0113) 2457011

The Elbow Room is one of those places you wish you'd thought of. And if you had you'd be raking it in by now instead of trudging through Briggate every morning to intercept calls from angry members of the public. Elbows is somewhere between a bar and a pool hall, the place engenders just enough of the pool hall to attract pool players, and enough bar to attract some talent – it's always full of fit birds and likewise a plentiful selection of suitable males. The main bar area and tables are separate so bad pool players need not suffer the shame of being observed, although reality TV could make a killing from filming the 2am crowd shuffling

the same balls around the table. They also serve good food and run superb offers on food/pool combos at the weekend.

Tue-Sat 12pm-2am, Sun 2pm-10.30pm
Mon 2pm-2am
Chicken club sarny £5.50
House wine: £7.50

Fudge

25-27 Assembly Street (0113) 234 3588

Exchange Quarter classic with cool music, an intimate open brick interior and plenty of space to get drunk and shake your ass. In between gathering crowds with your moves there'll be plenty of time to check out the attractive crowd of punters before deciding that none of them will fancy you anyway. On Wednesdays they run two for one offers, which in a classy joint like this, it would be rude not to take advantage of.

Mon-Sat 8pm-2am
Sun closed apart from monthly night
Perfect. House wine: £9.90

Hakuna Matata

Swinegate (0113) 243 3586

Some people think it's slightly off the beaten track, being as it's approximately 8 seconds walk from Call Lane, but if you can force yourself to that extra exertion then you'll be well rewarded. It's busy during the day with lunching suits from the nearby offices, and attracts a mixed crowd of up-for-it revellers in the evening. There are lots of events during the week, which are well worth a look, and it's available for private hire. An added

bonus is the very big screen telly behind the bar which means you can get a drink whilst not taking your eye off the footie – handy for getting that sixth pint in whilst witnessing the ferocious hatchet challenge that lead to Alan Smith's latest red card.

Mon-Sat 12pm-2am, closed Sun
Food: Mon-Sat 12pm-10pm
16oz steak £12.95 House wine: £11

Milo

10 Call Lane (0113) 245 7101

Everyone loves Milo, which is why the place is packed at a weekend, and pretty damned full throughout the week. Most nights you'll find a decent enough DJ spinning some tunes so you can experience the ambiance of a club without having to shell out an entrance fee. There is an upstairs area to house the inevitable overspill as the pre-clubland crowds gather before they attack their prey. The drinks are pricey and they don't accept cards (well, so they told us) so make sure you've got cash coming out of your ears before embarking on a night out.

Tue 5pm-11pm, Wed-Thu 5pm-1am
Fri 5pm-2am, Sat 12pm-2am
House wine: £10

Mook

Hirsts Yard (0113) 245 9967

The main contender for the cutest bar name in Leeds and short listed for the prize of best round-the-bar lighting. It's pretty small and not the easiest bar in the world to find (some never make it past neighbouring club Space), but it's got a great little atmosphere

HAKUNA MATATA

2 Briggate Leeds
0113 243 6454

and pulls the stylish crowd like sailors to a rum conference. DJs spin the funkiest tunes, though God knows how – the decks are suspended from the ceiling. A good selection of cocktails too, as well as fish finger butties on the menu for the next day's hangover.

Mon-Thu 12pm-11pm, Fri-Sat 12pm-12am, Sun 12pm-11pm
Food: as above
Fish finger butty £4 House wine: £11 (£7 happy hour)

MPV

5-8 Church Street, Kirkgate
(0113) 243 9486
Truly an unfathomable venue in all manner of ways. Most bars in Leeds that close down, stay down, but MPV, like a phoenix from the flames, comes back for another helping. We may never decide if it's a bar or a club, but

we can't ignore those crazy red Portakabins, juxtaposed inside with some delightful décor and gorgeous clientele. It's got a knack of attracting punters pied piper style from the centre to its remote location; despite the fact Leeds has oodles of other drinking holes to offer. Inexplicable? Well, yes, but we liked it before and we like it now, and that's all you kids need to know.

Norman

36 Call Lane (0113) 234 3988

Stormin' Norman is holding steady as one of the bars you just have to pay a visit to in Leeds, despite the fact that swanky new boys are popping up around every corner. Unlike a lot of 'style bars' that try too hard, Norman keeps it simple with funky diner style red seating, a tasty and barginous Japanese noodle menu and DJs at the weekends spinning hip hop and breaks. It still packs in the punters by the shovel load, though thankfully the fickle 'places to be seen in' crew have moved on to the next new bar leaving the more loyal drinkers behind.

Mon-Wed 12pm-1am, Thu-Sat 12pm-2am, Sun 1pm-10.30am
Food: Mon-Thu 12.30pm-8.30pm, Fri-Sat 12.30pm-8pm
Celebration noodles £6.75 House wine: £10

Northern Light

Cross York Street (0113) 243 6446

A former school house that's been converted into a huge and visually spectacular bar and restaurant. It's located 20 seconds away from The Calls, but has grown on the locals. It's heaving every weekend with queues reaching across the street. Once inside, the super chic punters are complemented by the Northern Light's fine looking interior

Cross York Street
Leeds
LS2 7EE
0113 243 6446

Mon 5pm-2am
Tue-Sat 12pm-2am

thenorthernlight

NORMAN

RESTAURANT BAR 36 CALL LANE LEEDS

BRING YOUR HEAD

where you can knock back a mixture of cocktails across two floors. The downstairs floor is converted as a restaurant during the day serving some delicious and quite reasonable locally sourced organic/Modern British food. See also restaurant section
Mon-Sat 12pm-10.30pm (restaurant)
Mon-Thu 12pm-12am, Fri-Sat 12pm-2am
Mon-Sat 9pm-2am (club, in term-time),
Thu-Sat 9pm-2am (club, out of term time)
2 courses for £10, 3 for £13
British rib eye beef £12.50
House wine: £9.50

Oporto
31-33 Call Lane (0113) 243 4008

Oporto was one of the original players in the Call Lane bar market. It opened long enough ago to not have to resort to trendy gimmicks in order to lure new customers. And now that Call Lane is the place to be on a Friday night and everyone else wishes they'd had the same idea, it ambles along, confident of its proven maternal status. Oporto attracts a loyal following and odd gaggle of pretentious folk, eager to point out they knew this place before it was cool. Just tell them

to piss off and get stuck into the top-notch food.
Mon-Tue 12pm-12am, Wed-Thu & Sat 12pm-1am, Fri 12pm-2am, Sun 1pm-12am
Food: Mon-Thu 12pm-10.30pm, Fri-Sat 12pm-10pm, Sun 1pm-5pm
Rib-eye steak £10 House wine: £10.50

Oslo
178 Lower Briggate (0113) 245 7768
Oslo is like a big warm cave, which is nice, if slightly surreal. It's like a sixties remake of Journey to the Centre of the Earth, but much cooler because there's beer and no volcanic activity. Expect to pay a lot of money for drinks, though you classy types will be pleased to see that they come on a fancy sliver tray, and you can get table service. It's an ideal place to show off how rich, cool and well-connected you are. Sitting next to Chris Moyles on the bus on the way into town doesn't count.
Wed-Thu 7pm-2am, Fri 8pm-4pm,
Sat 7pm-4am, Sun 8pm-2am
Cajan chicken panini £3 House wine: £13

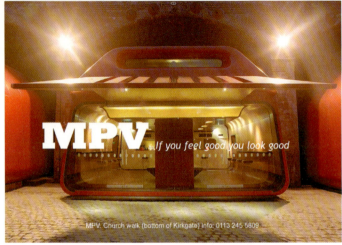

MPV ...If you feel good you look good

MPV. Church walk (bottom of Kirkgate) Info: 0113 245 5809

Reclaim
Calls Grill, 38 The Calls (0113) 245 3870
Stylish bar below The Calls Grill restaurant, Reclaim offers retro chic in cool surroundings with the interior decorated in vibrant colours and artwork made from reclaimed wood. The outside seating overlooking the river is a major bonus for soaking up rays in the summer months and the huge tables inside are great to cram a large group around. Save yourself a walk into town after dinner in the above restaurant or just pop in for snacks and drinks, and end up spending the whole night here, what with the regular midweek barbeques and DJs at the weekend. Tasty.
Mon-Sat 12pm 'til late, Sun 12pm-10.30pm

Revolution
48 Call Lane (0113) 243 2778

A bar that specialises in vodka? Now you're talking. Chocolate vodka, minty vodka and chilli vodka (for the hilarious pranksters amongst us), Revolution's enduring popular-

DRINK VODKA OR ELSE.

AND I WOULDN'T ARGUE IF I WERE YOU.
OVER 100 DIFFERENT VODKAS TO CHOOSE FROM AND SOME OF LEEDS'
BEST DJS 7 NIGHTS A WEEK. OPEN 'TIL 2AM THURSDAY, FRIDAY AND SATURDAY.
VODKA HEAVEN IS REVOLUTION IS VODKA HEAVEN.

48 CALL LANE ○ LEEDS ○ 0113 243 2778 ○ LEEDS@REVOLUTION-BARS.CO.UK ○ ALL RIGHTS RESERVED

RƎVOLUTION®

ity on Call Lane is thanks to its dedication to Russian potato juice, but also the hearty food and top DJs slamming vinyl in the evenings. Don't deny yourself the fun of buying huge rounds of vodka shots in a rush of inebriated generosity.

Mon-Sat 12pm-2am, Sun 1pm-12.30am
Food: Mon-Sun 12pm-6pm
Steak baguette £5.50 House wine: £9.50
Shots from £1.50

The Townhouse
Assembly Street (0113) 219 4006
Seems to have been around forever, but still showing no signs of dwindling in popularity, thanks to its ongoing reputation for attracting Leeds' beautiful people. Spread over three floors, there's a café bar on the ground floor with some decent food and the top floor is reminiscent of a small club. During the day there's a constant scramble for outdoor seating in the summer. At night, if you can get past the strict door policy (dress up to get in) it's a fine venue to sip rather expensive award-winning cocktails while drooling at the crowds of unobtainable beautiful drinkers. Available for private hire.

Mon-Sat 12pm-2am, Sun 12pm-10.30pm
Food: Mon-Sat 12pm-2am,
Sun 12pm-10.30pm
Thai chicken ciabatta £4 House wine: £9.95

eat in the   dance in the   drink in the   jazz in the

The Wardrobe

**6 St Peter's Building's, St Peter's Square
(0113) 383 8800**

Whilst many punters on a Friday night wander aimlessly into bars they're told are cool whether they want to be drinking there or not, the patrons of the Wardrobe saunter into this pit of cool for good reason. With an impressive cocktail menu (fellas, you might want to watch her on those...) and a live music programme to rival some of the bigger gig venues in the city (they have some form of live music every night), you'll never have a dull night in here. It's next to the new BBC building, in the rapidly trendifying arts corner of the city so the clientele are a little more laidback than the usual Call Lane rab-

ble. You'll not find your average Ben Sherman/short skirt/3 hour hairdo partygoer in here. How refreshing.
Mon-Wed 12pm-12am, Thu-Sat 12pm-1am

Bar Pacific
Swan Street (0113) 244 9130

Hidden away on an alleyway between Briggate and Lands Lane, Pacific's a fine venue for outdoor drinking that's lapped up by skiving office workers and lunching shoppers. It's always rammed when there's a show on at City Varieties, but also demands a look when on city centre drinking missions – the acoustic gigs on Thursday night offer a plausible excuse for midweek boozy action.
Mon-Wed 11am-11pm,
Thu-Sat 11am-1am, Sun 11am-10.30pm
Food: Mon-Sun 12pm-7pm
Steak ciabatta £5.25 House wine: £6.95

Fab Café
46 Woodhouse Lane (0113) 244 9009
Quirky bar/club on the corner next to Morrisons that's a shrine to all that's best in retro kitsch – daleks and Dangermouse abound alongside Carlsberg and alphabetti spaghetti. It all makes for a slightly garish but warm nostalgia that pulls in the nearby

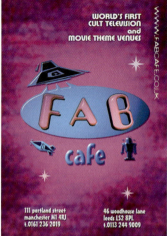

students, while the alternative tunes draw in an array of haircuts from the Leeds music scene. Worth a visit as it's hard not to have a good night in here and it deserves support for making a stand against all the mainstream chain bar townie crud surrounding it.
Mon-Sat 4.30pm-2am, Sun 4.30pm-
12.30am. Food: as above
Pot noodle £2.70 House wine: £1.70 gls

Life Bar ~~VK~~ VODKA KICK
44-48 The Headrow (0113) 245 2575
As the title suggests, they style themselves as a mature, yet trendy venue. Life bar experiments with the concept of blending a modern bar, club and eatery in to chic surroundings, and it works pretty well, especially with

FOOD DRNK MUSIC

MIXING TIN

9A ALBION STREET LEEDS LS1 5AA
0113 246 8899

phere making it an essential stop-off on a boozy night out. Regular cocktail competitions let the bar staff show off their tricks, and it's as good an excuse to get trashed as you'll need. They also serve great fresh home cooked food that's too tempting for most office workers who nip in at lunchtime, then stumble back half cut to afternoon meetings with hilarious consequences for the Leeds business economy.

Mon-Tue 12pm-11pm
Food: Mon-Thu 12pm-9pm, Fri-Sat till 7pm
Steak chilli & chips £4.50 House wine: £9.50

the toned down dancefloor providing an environment for weekend drinkers who might prefer bars to clubbing. Much care and attention is spent on creating a stylish interior – in particular the light shades, which would make MC Esher proud.

Mon 11am-2am, Tue-Wed 11am-11.30pm,
Thu-Sat 11am-2am, Sun 12pm-12.30am
Food: Mon-Sun 11am-9.30pm
Pork fillets £8.50 House wine: £9.95

Mixing Tin
14 Albion Arcade (0113) 246 8899
Cracking city centre bar that's dedicated to cocktails and rock music. It attracts a lot of regulars in the week and is always rammed at the weekend where there's a great atmos-

Room
Boar Lane (0113) 242 6161
Yet another swanky lounge bar/restaurant adding weight to the argument that Leeds is just soooo trying to be London. Dead posh, dead pricey and made for folk who get the shakes unless they have a Moet drip by their side. Live music and an outside courtyard save it from being too up itself, and the fine food is impossible to argue with. Damn.

Sun-Thu 12pm-11pm, Fri-Sat 12pm-2am
Food: Mon-Wed 12pm-2.30pm & 6pm-
10pm (Thu-Sun till 11pm)
Chicken maryland £14 House wine: £12

Just Drink It!

VODKA KICK

VK
VODKA
BLUE

www.clubvk.com

VK
VODKA KICK

Tiger Tiger
The Light, Albion Street (0113) 236 6999

With a climate like the one in Leeds, it's a pretty sensible idea to cater for customer's eating, drinking, dancing and dining requirements all under one roof. Here you're pretty much spoilt for choice where bars are concerned – it has five, as well as a stylish restaurant. All individually themed, you'll find a funky Moroccan kaz bar, a Canadian mountie's Lodge, and a 1920s style cocktail lounge, all offering an extensive bar and cocktail menu. For dancing into the small hours there are two dancefloors, and best of all, bar food is available 'til 2am – no need for the dodgy kebab whilst waiting for grumpy cabbies on the way home. Guest list and VIP entry a must – phone to request.

Mon–Sat 12pm-2am (Food throughout)
Chump of lamb £12.95 House wine: £10.95
(£5.75 happy hour)

Financial District

Baby Jupiter
11 York Place (0113) 242 1202

The height of retro cool, what used to be Soul Kitchen is now a den of 60s and 70s hip. Tiny though it is, it's packed full of inspired décor – purple velvet, orange fish bowl lights and film posters painted on the walls with a funky, soulful soundtrack to back it up. It's a bit out of the way but altogether a fab hangout – stylish, cool and retro chic, just like Jane Fonda in her Barbarella heyday. Yum.

Mon/Tue 12pm-7pm, Wed 12pm-8pm, Thu 12pm-11pm, Fri 12pm-late, Sat 7pm-late
Food: Mon-Fri 12pm-2.30pm
Spanish meatballs & patatas bravas £5
House wine: £10.50

Firefly
21 Park Row (0113) 243 1122

"What's this, my bank has become a trendy wine bar?". Well thank God for internet banking, as Firefly's arrival in the former Royal Bank of Scotland HQ sparked a rejuvenation in the financial district's bar and restaurant scene that Leeds had been waiting years for. This glowing creature has been attracting the city's bar butterflies in their swarms, with its plush dark wood and steel surroundings that are reminiscent of a Manhattan speak easy. It attracts an affluent midweek clientele, with a more chilled out collection of beautiful people at the weekend. With two bars split over two levels, the basement bar adopts a clubby vibe on Saturdays with DJs

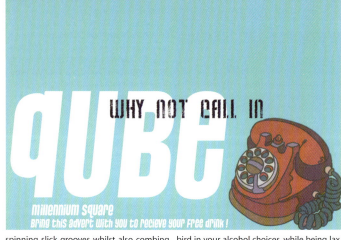

WHY NOT CALL IN qube

millennium square
Bring this advert with you to recieve your free drink !

spinning slick grooves whilst also combing one of Leeds' more unique quirks – a beer garden below street level. The upstairs bar is a fine spot to knock back an array of cocktails or grab a bite to eat from their brasserie menu – you'll be thrashing the expenses account in here until the small hours.

Brasserie & bar: Mon-Sat 12pm-11pm, Sun 12pm-10.30pm
Cocktail lounge: Thu-Sat 9pm-2am (avail. for private hire Sun-Wed)
Bar menu: 12pm-1am every day

Park

South Parade (0113) 244 0342

Despite all its grand designs at being a cocktail bar, Park is nothing more than a glorified pub. Not that it's a bad thing – the live music programme coupled with the impressive cocktail menu mean that you can be a classy bird in your alcohol choices, while being lax about your chosen footwear. It's a whole lot easier to get pissed on cosmopolitans while wearing trainers.

Mon-Tue 12pm-11pm, Wed-Thu 12pm-12am, Fri 12pm-2am, Sat 4pm-2am, Sun 4pm-10.30pm

Prohibition

Greek Street (0113) 224 0005

Of all the colours of the rainbow, this new venue chooses pretty much only one – black. This being the case, it's more a venue for classy evening cocktails rather than a lunchtime salad (you'd have trouble seeing it for a start). Massive, modern and moody.

Mon-Wed 12pm-12am, Thu 12pm-1am, Fri-Sat 12pm-2am, Sun 12pm-12am
Food: Mon-Sun 12pm-10pm
Chicken salad £6.95 House wine: £10.50

Millennium Square

Bourbon

43-51 Cookridge Street (0113) 2441703
Named after the biscuit, but they also sell the biscuit. It's cheap, very popular with students and there's some decent DJs at the weekend. The daily 2-4-1 on drinks before 8pm is dangerously close to alcohol suicide.
Mon-Thu 12pm-12am, Fri-Sat 12pm-2am,
Sun 12pm-10pm
Cajun chicken baguette £4.50
House wine: £8

Qube ~~VK VODKA KICK~~

Millennium Square (0113) 234 3777

Huge bar on Millennium Square that's an essential stop off en route to Creation, Baja and Bourbon etc. The enormous patio makes for some fun outdoor drinking, and the late openings at weekends means you can soak up moonlight as easily as the sun's rays whilst getting sloshed. There's decent food served 'til late and you can nearly always get a table.
Mon-Wed 11am-1am, Thu-Sat 11am-2am,
Sun 12pm-12.30am
Food: Mon-Wed 12pm-12am, Thu-Sat
12pm-1am, Sun 12pm-11.30pm
Chicken panini £3.25 House wine: £9.95

Northern Quarter

Isis

12 Merrion Street (0113) 242 9020
Remaining busy at the weekend as an overflow to Mojo, this is a calmer and swankier bedfellow to its gritty rock 'n' roll neighbour. Isis is all foreign beers, muted décor and plush leather sofas. It's pricey and they have a bad habit of inviting live DJs with flagrant disregard for the size of the place.
Mon-Wed 5pm-1am, Thu-Sat 5pm-2am
House wine: £10.50

Mojo

18 Merrion Street (no phone)
It's small, they don't serve any draft beers, it's nearly impossible to get a seat, but still Mojo is unquestionably one of the best bars in Leeds. There's a fantastic music policy (no repetitive beats, lots of guitars), a huge array of super strong cocktails, and an up-for-it atmosphere that always makes you think something big is going to happen. Your chances of squeezing in after 9pm at the weekend are pretty slim, so you may have to idle away a few Friday nights kicking your heels in its next door waiting room, Isis.
Mon-Wed 6pm-11pm, Thu 6pm-12am,
Fri-Sat 6pm-1am
House wine: £8.50

5/5a Cross Belgrave Street Leeds
0113 3050372 barsandinista@hotmail.com

Cantina bar

Sandinista!
Cantina bar

North Bar

24 New Briggate (0113) 242 4540

Cool Leeds bar crammed into a space the size of my hallway (I do live in a mansion), North attracts a chilled out alternative crowd. Their dedication to European beers goes down a treat with the great selection of bar snacks and one glass quickly leads to two, so it's a blessing there's no space left for falling over after too much super strength Duval. The bar's also notable for hosting artwork from talented local artists, so you get something interesting to look at whilst standing around pining for a chair.

Mon-Tue 12pm-1am, Wed-Sat 12pm-2am, Sun 12pm-10.30pm (food throughout)
Paninis £3.50 House wine: £10

Sandinista!

5 Cross Belgrave Street (0113) 305 0372

A bar that shares its name with a Clash Album and group of Nicaraguan revolutionaries would have to be somewhere pretty damn cool and it's good to know that Sandinista! doesn't disappoint. Hispanically styled, it's just the place if you're up for an evening of beers and cocktails with mates, followed by an attempt at dancing along to the to the eclectic tunes played by weekend DJs. The food menu is far more impressive than your usual bar fodder, and the pick and mix sandwich menu is the perfect hangover cure. You're sure going to need it after all those cocktails Gringo!

Food: Mon-Sun 12pm-10pm
Chicken & pesto mash £5.95
House wine: £10

Headingley

The Arc

19 Ash Road (0113) 275 2223

The success of this Headingley super-bar confirmed the huge market for posh places in student centralis. The wealthy students had grown thin on steak flavoured McCoys, and

It's what's inside that counts

yearned for spicy ciabattas and shiny stairs. And lo, the Arc was born. Competition from Trio and Box (ironically owned by the same company) hasn't really harmed its popularity but the food does seem to have gone a bit ropey - maybe they're getting complacent?

Mon-Wed 11am-11pm, Thu-Sat 11am-12pm, Sun 11am-10pm
Food: Mon-Sat 11am-10pm, Sun till 9pm
Tagliatelle £6.45 House wine: £8.50

The Box
8 Otley Road (0113) 224 9266

It's never going to topple the Oak in the summer drinking stakes but the fully opening front wall means you can drink outside while sitting inside and enjoy the fumes of one of Britain's busiest streets. If you use your imagination there's a bit of a Scandinavian snow lodge thing going on inside, though the TV screens, pool tables and lack of St Bernard's get in the way a bit.

Mon-Fri 10am-11pm, Sat 10am-1am
Sun 10am-12.30am. Food: 10am-8pm
Big breakfast £4.75 House wine: £8.50

Trio
44 North Lane (0113) 203 6090

Without doubt the coolest bar in Headingley, with its tropical late night lounge theme. You'll find cocktails, foreign beer, an upstairs restaurant and funky tunes which all serve to give it the feel of a trendy Rat Pack style hangout. Slightly pricier than most other watering holes in LS6, but those suede booths must throw up quite a cleaning bill…

Mon-Sat 5pm-11pm, Sun 5pm-10.30pm
Food: Mon-Fri 12pm-3pm & 6pm-11pm,
Sat-Sun 12pm-11pm
Wood fired pizza £6.50 House wine: £9.50

pubs

www.itchyleeds.co.uk

highlights

- Whitelock's – pubs like they should be
- The Oak beer garden in summer

lowlights

- Refurbs gone wrong at the Scarborough Hotel
- Being within 50 yards of Break For The Border
- Edwards. Urgghhh.

Opening hrs: Mon-Sat 11am-11pm, Sun 12pm-10.30pm unless otherwise stated

Exchange Quarter

Aire
32 The Calls (0113) 203 1811
Hidden away down in the trendy Calls you're as likely to come here for the stunning river views as you are the booze. Short of watching England get beaten in the cricket again, this is what a Leeds summer is all about. Blissful. Rubbish food though.
Food: Mon-Sun 12pm-5.30pm

Break For The Border
174-178 Briggate (0113) 244 2666
Take this place literally and next time you feel the allure of this place, leg it to the next county. Gone are the days when all the kids

wanted was cheap plonk on tap and enough room to swing a fist and flash some unsupported bossoms. It sells booze, but that, quite honestly, is about all it has going for it.
Mon-Wed 5pm-11pm, Thu 12pm-11pm, Fri-Sat 12pm-2am, Sun 6pm-11pm
Food: Mon-Sun 12pm-11pm

Millennium Square

O'Neill's
Great George Street (0113) 244 0810

Amazingly, O'Neill's is the only Irish theme pub left in central Leeds. Better still, some actual live Irish people have been known to drink here. Does this mean the Guinness tastes better than in other pubs? No. Does it annoy the bar staff to be constantly asked where they're from then watch you look blank and say 'Oh, is that near Dublin?' Yes, so please stop it.

Mon-Thu 11.30am-11pm, Fri-Sat 11.30am-12am, Sun 12pm-10.30pm
Food: Sun-Thu 11.30am/12pm-9pm, Fri-Sat 11.30am-7pm

Barracuda Bar
20 Woodhouse Lane (0113) 244 1212

The once South African sports bar has had quite a makeover since their parent company was bought out by Barracuda Bars Ltd – yup they've changed the name. Which won't really affect you to be honest because you you can still see as much rugby, football and cricket as your heart desires on their multitude of televisions, the drinks remain cheap and they still play cheesy tunes in the evening. Barracuda's not for everyone, but what they do, they do well. There's a strong

Best Proper Boozers
Whitelocks
The Original Oak
The Fenton
The Grove
The Packhorse
Victoria Commercial Hotel

Ford**Fiesta**

chance that the venue will change a lot more over the ensuing months as the transition is felt – in which case can I buy those massive ceiling high cricket stumps please?

Mon-Wed 11am-11pm, Thu 11am-12am, Fri-Sat 11am-2am, Sun 12pm-11pm
Food: Mon-Sat 11am-6pm, Sun 12pm-6pm

Walkabout
Cookridge Street (0113) 205 6500

The final venue (debatably) for the Otley Run, Walkabout is well suited to the task. For a start you can't fail to see, hear, or smell it from Woodhouse Lane. The evening clientele consists primarily of pissed-up pub crawlers, university rugby players, women of a certain age wearing their daughter's leather trousers and girls of a certain age wearing their mum's make-up. Oh, and as many Australian backpackers as Leeds has managed to attract that week. If you're not drunk already, don't go.

Mon 11am-11pm, Tue 11am-12am, Thu 11am-1am, Wed & Fri-Sat 11am-2am
Food: Mon 11am-10pm, Tue 11am-11pm, Wed 11am-1am, Thu 11am-12am, Fri-Sat 11am-1am

Victoria Commercial Hotel
Great George Street (0113) 246 1386

Fantastic traditional boozer, and one of the oldest pubs in the city – reinforcing the idea that things were better in the old days. This proper Yorkshire boozer serves several regional ales on tap and does reasonable food at lunchtime all served up in a huge main room the size of Queen Vic's bath chair. The staff are friendly, and the warm atmosphere will have you yearning for the simple pleasures of yesteryear – you'll probably go home and bath yourself in the kitchen sink.
Mon-Sat 11.30am-11pm, Sun closed
Food: Mon-Sat 12pm-7pm

City Centre

The Angel Inn
Angel Inn Yard (0113) 245 1428

Tucked away down a back alley in the heart of the city, The Angel is a cosy and lively affair tastefully decked out and impeccably clean. Being a Sam Smiths pub, the bar is geared towards proper pub drinking and features a bevy of hand-pulled ales.

Southerners and girls are humoured with a wide range of alcopops and wine. Everybody's happy. The food's good, if a tad basic, but it's a pub not a bloody restaurant. A prime stop-off for a breather during a shopping spree, with plenty of outside seating for drinking al fresco come the summer, like what they do on the continent.
Food: Mon-Fri 12pm-3pm & 5pm-7pm,
Sat 12pm-7pm, Sun 12pm-2.30pm

Edwards
Merrion Street (0113) 246 9297

Neatly nestled within the Merrion Centre, alongside enough pound shops to make a pikey cry and Morrissons. If you still insist on going here wear man-made fibers and eau-de-chips and you'll fit in just fine.
Mon-Thu 11am-11pm, Fri-Sat 11am-12am, Sun 12pm-10.30pm

The Grove Inn
Back Row (0113) 243 9254

Now this is our kind of place. If you really want to discover what devastatingly attractive and knowledgeable people us itchy folk are then get yourself down here sharpish. But if proper old pubs aren't your thing, then please stay away – we don't want any Wetherspoons riff-raff in here to take the shine off our after-work pints thank you very much. Apart from the astonishingly charismatic clientele, here's the place to catch some quality jazz, blues, folk and unplugged talent while supping on a tasty guest beer.
Mon-Sat 12pm-11pm, Sun 12pm-10.30pm
Food: Mon-Fri 12pm-2pm, Sun 1pm-3pm

Water, barley malt and hops, nothing else

Playing Pool

Elbow Room
Citrus
Northern Snooker Centre
The Box
The Skyrack

Ford**Fiesta**

The Guildford
115 The Headrow (0113) 244 9204

Helen Keller has not yet been round to redecorate this pub; the same cannot be said for most of the former proper boozers in the city centre. Probably one of only a handful of bonafide old school drinking holes left in the city centre, The Guildford's just made for sipping on a few afternoon pints, chomping on some peanuts, filling the entire building with cigarette smoke and browsing over The Racing Post. Worth a visit not so much for a mingle with the regulars, but just so that you remember what a 'pub' looks like before they all get massacred in an imminent interior design frenzy.
Food: Mon-Sat 12pm-3pm

Joseph's Well
Hanover Walk (0113) 245 0875

Although Joseph's Well is primarily a live venue, there's a vibe in the pub section as well. Most of the bands drink in here from time to time but since it's nobody's local

(well, apart from a handful of office monkeys in the early evening), the crowd keeps changing. Don't expect to rub shoulders with any up-and-coming stars – not that there aren't any, it's just that the ones with any prospect of fame won't be hanging with the likes of you. Open 'til midnight most nights, which gives you that bit of extra time to drink away your sorrow when you realise you'll never be/get to shag Julian Casablancas.
Mon-Fri 12pm-12am, Sat 5pm-12am, Sun 12pm-10.30pm
Food: Mon-Sun 12pm-2pm

Scarborough Hotel
Bishopgate Street (0113) 243 4590

We're getting a bit bored of saying this but here you'll find another case of the ooh what a surprise, faceless, tasteless pub co invasion. Identikit Boozers Inc has rocked up, flashed a bit of cash and mercilessly ripped the soul out of a once decent skanky boozer, thrown it on the floor, kicked it around a bit and left it in the gutter. The end.
Food: Mon-Sat 11am-7pm,
Sun 12pm-7pm

soiree / swarer / n. evening party esp. for conversation or music
SOIREE
AT THE SQUARE
COME AND SAMPLE OUR RELAXED ATMOSPHERE AND A SOUNDTRACK OF NEW & CLASSIC R'N'B PLAYED BY DJ
LEE WRIGHT
(RADIO AIRE SMOOTH GROOVES)
96.3 radio aire
SPECIAL DRINKS PROMOTIONS
COCKTAILS 2-4-£5
2 FULL SPIRIT MEASURES
3 SHOOTERS 4 THE PRICE OF 2
OFFICIAL PRE-BAR FOR Coffy @ REHAB
TIME: 7.30 TIL LATE / DRESS CODE: SMART
'COOL MUSIC FOR HOT CITY NIGHTS'
THURSDAYS
SQUARE ON THE LANE. 58-63 BOAR LANE, LS1 6HW. T: 0113 246011

Squares
58-63 Boar Lane (0113) 246 0111
Frankly my feet hurt from standing up in cramped, trendy wine bars too long. What I need is somewhere I can have a seat, drink some cocktails (of the larger than a shot glass kind) and eat some decent pub food without feeling like my H&M jeans are being scrutinised by beady eyed fashionistas. Squares might be avoided by some, but with some funky mid week tunage, enough room to have a barn dance in and staff who actually smile at you when you order a drink, it's a very decent choice by all accounts. And their Premiership coverage on those crazy screens keeps everyone's boyfriend happy, what more could you ask for?
Mon-Sun 11am-11pm
Food: Mon-Sat 11am-7pm Sun 'til 5.30pm

Stick Or Twist
Merrion Way (0113) 234 9748
Erm, neither please. I'm off to drink somewhere less shit. It's a bit skanky and another one of those Wetherspoon places we all love to loathe and the only real reason to be in here is when you've just lost everything bar your last 99p in the casino next door and need a cheap beer.
Food: 10am-10.30pm, Sun 12pm-9.30pm

Whitelock's
Turks Head Yard (Off Briggate)
(0113) 245 3950
Now this is what I like to see, a place where you can absorb a bit of bygone culture while getting shit-faced at the same time. Hidden away down an alley in the centre of town (so the pigeons can't find it – they are rather fond of bitter and salt and vinegar crisps), the building dates from the 18th century and is a haven of old worldy charm. It's the kind of place that tourists would love (if they could ever find it), what with its fine selection of beers and tasty sarnies.
Food: Mon-Sun 12pm-7pm

University Area

Dry Dock   ~~VK~~ VODKA KICK
Woodhouse Lane (0113) 203 1841

Essentially the Leeds Met equivalent of The Fav, the infamous barge is a staple for lunchtime drinkers. Americans can stick their groundhogs – over here we know it's summer when after sweating indoors throughout the April/May heatwave, Dry Dock finally opens its top deck and lets the happy punters sit outside in time for the northern monsoon season. As the only late bar round here (we're not counting Walkabout and Barracuda as proper options) it inevitably fills when the neighbouring pubs call time.
Mon-Sat 12pm-1am, Sun 12pm-12am
Food: Mon-Sun 12pm-6pm

The Faversham VK
Springfield Mount (0113) 243 1481
Dangerously, temptingly, almost obscenely close to the Leeds uni lecture blocks. The Faversham just sits there after those one o'clock lectures, looking all funny at you, making the voices in your head start whispering 'what harm can a little drink do?'. Perhaps schizophrenia and latent alcoholism aren't the only reasons for Fav's popularity, but they're as good as any, damnit. Friday night is the sensationally messy 'Quid's In,' where alcopops and the less palatable beers are a mere £1. Chaos.
Mon-Thu 11am-11pm, Fri-Sat 11am-2am, Sun 12pm-12.30am
Food: Mon-Sat 12pm-7pm

The Fenton VK VODKA KICK
Woodhouse Lane (0113) 245 3908
Ahhh, they don't make them like this any more. Real ale, a bit smelly and patronised by a healthy balance of proper old soaks, students and university lecturers (compare and contrast), The Fenton has it all. There's a pool table and jukebox providing in-house entertainment and live bands in the upstairs room at weekends. Gigs are hit and miss depending on the quality of the PA bands care to bring along with them. Of course, this is also a stalwart of the latter stages of the Otley Run.
Mon-Fri 11.30am-11pm, Sat 12pm-11pm, Sun 12pm-10.30pm
Food: Mon-Thu 11.30am-7pm, Fri-Sat 12pm-4pm

The Library VK VODKA KICK
229 Woodhouse Lane (0113) 244 0794
'It's a Scream' kids! Right, so what is 'a scream' exactly? Could it be the sound of a load of parched students excitingly waving their yellow cards in the faces of the bar staff in the hope of securing some cut-price booze? Or is it the screams of laughter that arise from 'Hiya Dad, honestly, I'm in the library' style gags? Or is it the inward screams of boredom that arise from spending an afternoon in here? It's big, it sells booze and does some food to keep the energy levels up – but enough about the good points, 'Scream' was the title of a horror film you know.
Food: Mon-Sun 12pm-5pm

The Pack Horse VK
208 Woodhouse Lane (0113) 245 3980
Packing 'em in since 1904 (or whenever), the Horse is a refurb waiting to happen (since it's one of the only proper pubs left in the vicinity), but if the fateful day ever came, the good folk of Leeds would come out in their thousands to beat the decorators with sticks. This place is perfect as it is, what with smoky little

rooms made for long afternoon sessions, a pool table for impromptu sporting tournaments and a sterling gig venue upstairs.
Food: Mon-Sat 12pm-7pm

Headingley/Hyde Park Area

Headingley Taps VK
North Lane (0113) 220 0931

Not as famous as The Oak or the 'Rack, but still bloody brilliant. The Taps serves up a decent Sunday lunch, a weekly quiz (Tuesdays) and a proper pint or two. Also the big screen tellies, fit bar staff, and Sunday karaoke provide an extra pull, while the monthly live sets from DJ Wandering Hans are not to be missed.
*Food: Mon-Fri 11am-7pm,
Sat-Sun 11am-5.30pm*

Hyde Park VK VODKA KICK
Hyde Park Corner (0113) 274 5597

Naff décor, badly modernised and full of students chatting about what they chatted about in the library all day. It shows the footy and offers up a half-baked attempt at outside seating for those of you who like a bit of eau de traffic fume with your pint.
*Food: Mon-Fri 12pm-7pm,
Sat-Sun 12pm-5pm*

Hyde Park Social Club
Hyde Park (too pikey to have a phone)

Craftily situated in the heart of Hyde Park's rat-infested budget housing area, it may not be pretty but it's much more fun than sitting at home listening to the pipes leak and wondering if the asbestos-fuelled creature living in the roof space has grown enough to come down and eat you. Cheap beer and pool tho'.

New Inn
68 Otley Road (0113) 224 9131

An honest to goodness public house with outside seating for summer boozing. The stone floors and wooden furniture give it a homely kind of feel, and if you get down there on a Sunday and have a stab at one of their tasty Sunday dinners, you can almost imagine you're back at the parent's gaff getting your washing done again. Aaah, bliss…

The Original Oak
2 Otley Road (0113) 275 1322

Pulling in the punters all year round and toasting them rotten in the summer sunshine in its world famous beer garden (doubling as a campsite for nomadic Aussies when the cricket's on), The Oak has secured its reputation as Headingley's premier drinking hole since the Skyrack lost its grip. With barbecues in summer, comedy every Thursday, ace Sunday roasts and loads of screens for footy and rugby watching, you've pretty much got everything you need for a week's worth of entertainment. Heck, even the Aussie cricket team have drunk here – we're definitely onto a winner.
*Food: Mon-Fri 12pm-7pm, Sat 12pm-5pm,
Sun 12pm-4pm*

The Royal Park
Queens Road (0113) 275 7494

Hidden away deep in the Bronx (well, next to Baraka so it shouldn't be that hard to find), this is strictly a locals and students kind of place. A massive pub with pool tables upstairs and a dingy gig venue in the basement, it has just been made over, but in a good way having still kept the traditional vibe in some of the smaller rooms. Not the traditional ale and pork scratching type of boozer, but not one of those identity crisis pubs that thinks it's a bar either. All good.
Food: Mon-Fri 5pm-8pm, Sat-Sun 12pm-4pm & 5pm-8pm

The Skyrack
2 Otley Road (0113) 278 1519

As one of Headingley's old skool big guns, the 'Rack draws in the hordes in much the same way as its adversary on the other side of the road, The Original Oak. However, whereas the Oak is regarded as a 'local', the Skyrack is mainly a stop for the pub crawlers and sports socialisers to neck the required quota before going somewhere more worthwhile. Not everyone's cup of tea, but nonetheless an integral part of the Headingley experience.
Mon-Tue 11am-11pm, Wed-Sat 11am-12.30am, Sun 12pm12.30pm
Food: Mon-Sun 12pm-7pm

Three Horseshoes
98 Otley Road (0113) 275 7222

Horses are distressingly scarce in Leeds these days, but if you're cantering through Far Headingley and accidentally lose a shoe, this is a fine place to rest your tired hooves. There's decent food, very pretty bar staff and ridiculously cheap booze. No really, it's so cheap. If you're a student staying in Oxley Hall you'll be looking at a low third class degree at best, as you'll be always in here. 15 pints of Tetley's will set you back approximately 9 sheets (possibly a bit more, but not much) – which is the drinking equivalent of incitement to riot. Cool.
Food: Mon-Fri 12pm-8pm, Sun 12pm-4pm

Woodies ~~VK~~ VODKA KICK
104 Otley Road (0113) 278 4393

The birthplace of the Otley Run and so we'll show our respect. Damning with faint praise might even be pushing it, but here goes: it serves a variety of booze (beers, wines and spirits); the roof doesn't leak (handy in the winter); I've never seen a fight in there; and, by simple logic, it's got to be someone's local. It's a nice enough place to drink, in the same way that Guernsey is a nice enough place to visit. It just isn't strictly necessary.
Food: Mon-Sat 12pm-2pm

Free
every
Saturday?

Free every Saturday

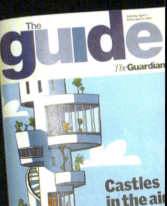

clubs

www.itchyleeds.co.uk

highlights

- Movin' on up at HiFi
- Drum and bassing it at Space
- Finding your indie soul at Think Tank
- Mid-week drinks deals at every cheesy club
- Busy clubs every night iof the week
- Semi-naked staff at Baja Beach Club

lowlights

- Finding the cash machine at Creation
- Communal sweat baths at Heaven and Hell
- Bumping into your mum at Flares
- Bumping into your dad at The Birdcage
- Semi-naked staff at Baja Beach Club
- Taxi getting (book one or hide in a hotel foyer

All times and admissions are approximations – club nights change and vary faster than we can keep up with for an annual guide… check itchyleeds.co.uk or call ahead to be certain that the night you're after is on.

Atrium
6 Grand Arcade (0113) 242 6116

It's been around a while now serving up some three-floored clubby, bary, loungy laidback underground disco, RnB, soul with the odd jazzy soul band thrown in for good measure. Spread over three levels with different tuneage and different degrees of chilled. *Mon-Thu 9pm-2am, Fri 8.30pm-3am, Sat 10am-3am, £3-£5*

Baja Beach Club
43a Woodhouse Lane (0113) 245 4088

In the wake of the Rat and Parrot, I guess the good folk of Leeds had hoped for something a little up-scale from the soulless chain of shit-ness they'd come to know and well, know. Instead they got Baja Beach Club – comedy plastic sharks, a contrived sense of ker-razy fun and the obligatory selection of pissed-up students pretending to find it all a bit ironic. *Mon, Wed & Thu 9pm-2am, Tue 9.30pm-2.30am, Fri-Sat 8pm-2.30am, Sun 9pm-1am. Free b4 10pm, £3-£5 after*

Bar Phono
16 The Merrion Centre (0113) 242 9222

Bar Phono, despite its weird shopping centre location, manages to pack in the punters for a plentiful range of specialist nights. Check out the hardcore goth nights where you'll find multi-pierced, green-haired teenagers with specially adapted vampire teeth being sneered at for being too conventional. *Wed 10pm-2am, Thu 10pm-2am, Fri-Sat 9.30pm-2.30am, Sun 7pm-12am Wed £2-£4, Thu-Fri £2-£3, Sat £1-£4, Sun £10 (1 year's membership)*

The Birdcage   VK VODKA KICK
52-56 Boar Lane (0113) 246 7273

Calling this place a club is a bit like calling one of those Bernard Matthew's meat-a-likes a Sunday roast. The Birdcage is reminis-cent of being left at the entrance of the bingo while your gran chats up the balding compere. It's the kind of place where a ren-dition of 'Hi Ho Silver Lining' turns into a full on sing-song and you expect to see that singer from 'Cruise Ship' thrilling the audi-ence with her 'charms'. Astounding comedy potential though – if you're looking for somewhere to dance like a twat and end up with your trousers round your ankles, no-one will bat an eyelid if you do it here. *Wed-Thu 9pm-2am, Fri-Sat 8pm-3am, Sun 9pm-1am Wed 80p, Thu 90p b4 9.30pm, £2 after, Fri-Sat free b4 9pm, £3 b4 10.30pm, £6 after*

Bondi Beach Bar   VK VODKA KICK
City Square (0113) 243 4733

It began in tragedy. Where would the cheap-end clubbers find a revolving dance floor now that Planet Earth has crashed and burned? Luckily Bondi Beach Bar was quick to provide a brand new spinning floor and it's a mark-up on the old one – you don't have to all get off and push it past 1.30am. They've also gutted the seedy interior and rebuilt it from scratch. Although they've retained the surreal cabaret of the former Planet, bikini clad 'tub' girls are an additional feature, and obviously add a welcome touch of sophistication. *Mon-Sat 5pm-2.30am, Sun 5pm-10.30pm Mon-Wed free b4 11pm, £2 after, Thu £5/£4, Fri-Sat £2 b4 10pm, £3 b4 11pm, £5 after*

The Cockpit
Swinegate (0113) 244 1573

The Cockpit fills a much needed niche for indie of the more mainstream variety. It doesn't have the hidden gem status of your average shoe-gazing hangout but makes up for this by sheer size and crowd pulling potential. The down-at-heel interior and carefully selected bands/music policy keeps the kids happy in an angst-ridden, moody, foot-stamping kind of way.

Bar: Mon-Sat 4.30pm-11pm,
Tue 10.30pm-2.15am,
Thu-Fri 11pm-2.30am, Sat 11pm-3am
Tue £3, Thu £2.50/£3.50, Fri-Sat £4/£5

Club Paradise
39 New York Street (0113) 245 1555

Fluid has finally decided to close its doors after realising that no-one actually knew it existed, to be replaced quicker than you can say 'bunch of gurning monkeys' by spangly new boy, Club Paradise. A massive refurb and complete change of staff, doormen and DJs has changed this venue from a poor excuse for a party palace to a shining new club pit attracting DJs like Brandon Bloc and Judge Jules. 'Kahuna' and 'Love To Be' are its main nights pulling in a dedicated house crowd.

Thu 9pm-3am, Fri-Sat 10pm-4am
£5-£10

Creation
52 Cookridge Street (0113) 224 0100

The formula for Creation is roughly this: enter appalled at the boring music, company and atmosphere. Proceed to down untold quantities of cheap alcohol just to try and get yourself going. Indulge in the kind of evening which would make you teetotal if anyone was cruel enough to film you. We've all been to clubs like this – usually on a work night - and we've all sworn never to go again. We can only reiterate the logic of this sentiment.

Mon-Thu 5pm-2am, Fri-Sat 5pm-3am,
Sun 5pm-1am
£4-£8

The Elbow Room
64 Call Lane (0113) 245 7011

A bit of a multi-tasker, The Elbow Room's dalliance in the club scene often gets overlooked, but with nights like the 'Sugarbeat Club' on a Saturday night, those who dismiss it as merely a pool hall are fools. Featuring the talents of DJs Tim and Jez (of Utah Saints fame), it's rightfully building a reputation for itself with its mix of old school funk, hip hop and new school beats, and high calibre guests. It's roomy enough for a spot of dancing, yet intimate enough to give it that too-cool-for-school feel. And with entrance prices remaining low, you'll be on to an absolute winner, even if you are crap at pool.
Mon-Sat 12pm-2am, Sun 2pm-10.30pm
Sun-Fri free, Sat £5 after 10pm

Evolution VK VODKA KICK
Cardigan Fields, Kirkstall
(0113) 263 2632

Leeds largest nightclub serves its customers up a diet of quality tunes, decent drinks offers and plush surroundings. Many might dismiss the whole lot as a load of cheese, but this super club hosts a variety of quality nights which cater for a variety of music tastes including dance, RnB, house and party. Flagship nights 'Sundissential', 'Jelly Baby' and Monday's 'National Student Night' keep the punters flooding in, while its unique 360-degree cinema wall and seven bars keeps them perfectly occupied in between breaks from the dancefloor. Evolution, you are frankly spoiling us…
Mon-Tue & Thu-Sat 10pm-2.30am,
monthly Sun 2pm-12am
Mon £3/£4, Tue £10/£12, Thu/Fri £4/£5,
Sat £3/£5, Sun £15/£18

Federation @ Granary Wharf
The Leeds clubbing massive aren't quite as mental as the likes of the Sheffield 'Crasher brigade, or they weren't until the arrival of Federation. Held in the Dark Arches of Granary Wharf once a month, with a distinctly gay vibe, you'll find up-for-it revellers, pumping tunes, in-your-face décor, stilt-walkers, dancers in cages, and a parade through the streets of Leeds at the start of the night recruiting party people a la Manumission's efforts in fair Ibiza.
First Sat of month 10pm-4am. £10

No additives

Leeds Largest Night Club

evolution

MONDAYS : DRINK LIKE A FISH
The Famous National Student Night! Fun and Games with
the Monday Night Challenge and Drinks from £1!

DRINK LIKE
A FISH!

TUESDAYS : GET FU¥K 'D!
All you can drink! £10 NUS/MEMBERS £12 OTHERS!
Drink for Free all night, with all the top drink brands!

THURSDAYS : ♥R'n'B &♥FUNKY HOUS
The UK's Sexiest RnB Show! Playing Pure Sexy RnB and Funk
House for the sexiest boys and girls in Leeds.

www.clubevolution.co.u

GET BUSY & RETROSPEKT : FRIDAYS
Room 1 - Bass Line House & Classic Club Anthems
Room 2 - The Sexiest Soul, Hip-Hop & R'n'B (Brandy & Mix £2)

 Galaxy 105
OUT THERE

JELLY BABY : SATURDAYS
Three Rooms of the Best Dance, R'n'B and Party,
Pure Music & Entertainment with Galaxy 105 Drinks from £1.50

SUNDISSENTIAL : SUNDAYS
Monthly 10 Hour Hard House Event with Special Guest DJs
For Dates See clubevolution.co.uk

Evolution Nightclub. Cardigan Fields. Kirkstall. Leeds. LS4 2
Call: 0113 263 2632 / Over 18 / ROAR / Offers Subject to Change.

Flares VK VODKA KICK
40 Boar Lane (0113) 205 1931

Yet another ker-azy 70s themed venue, which without wishing to sound snobby, it's a bit common. The clientele do the usual cycle through the traditional club fluids – alcohol, spit exchanging, chucking up in the loos. Mind you it's the favourite venue of all the air stewardesses at Leeds Bradford Airport that I've spoken too, so your chances of guaranteed kop off action and possibly cheap air fares are all but guaranteed. Flares also shot to national fame because its UV lights gave people sun burn – I remember the days when condoms were enough protection for a night out.
Mon-Wed 8pm-12am, Thu 8pm-1am,
Fri-Sat 7pm-2am, Sun 7pm-12am
Mon-Thu & Sun Free,
Fri-Sat £3 after 10.30pm

The Fruit Cupboard VK
50-52 Call Lane (0113) 243 8666

Make up your mind on the name fellas. Briefly re-named as RPM last year, the Fruit Cupboard provides a shady little niche for

dedicated disco bunnies to shake their thang on the bite-sized dance floor. They do the hip hop and breakbeat thing to perfection and generally offer a laid-back night out. Although the bouncers can get bizarrely irate if you move the chairs.
Mon 9.30pm-2.30am, Tue 10pm-2.30am,
Thu-Fri 10pm-late, Sat 10.30pm-4am
Mon 80p, Tue £2, Thu-Fri £4-£5, Sat £6-£8

Heaven and Hell VK VODKA KICK
Grand Arcade (0113) 243 9963

And lo, there was neon revolving light, and a club with its own sustainable eco system. No really, Heaven and Hell actually does per-

form its own little climatic cycle, condensing the sweat of overheated clubbers so it can rain down on them, in hot, scummy drops. And yes, this is even more unpleasant than it sounds. Heaven and Hell is three floors of, lary, pissed-up clubbing at its sweaty best.
Mon-Wed 9pm-2am, Thu 9pm-3am,
Fri-Sat 10pm-4am
Mon-Wed £3-£6, Thu 80p b4 11pm, £3
after, Fri £10, Sat £12/£10

Club Listings? Go to www.itchycity.co.uk

MAJESTYK

ALWAYS STUDENT FRIENDLY

OPEN FRESHERS WEEK
MONDAY, TUESDAY, THURSDAY, FRIDAY & SATURDA

ADMISSION FRESHERS WEEK

MONDAY/THURSDAY - FREE B4 12PM / £3.50 AFTER
TUESDAY - NUS £2.50 B4 11PM / £3.50 AFTER

SELECTED DRINKS 50P B4 10.30PM*
£1 B4 11PM & 1.50 AFTER*
MONDAY, TUESDAY & THURSDAY ONLY

WWW.MAJESTYK.CO.UK

JUMPIN JAKS

"IF YOU CAN'T SING I
WE DON'T PLAY IT"
TEL: 0113 242 4333
PICK UP A FLYER FOR MORE DETAI

JAKS OPEN: TUESDAY, THURSDAY, FRIDAY, SATURDAY, SUND

MAJESTYK / JUMPIN' JAKS / CITY SQUARE / LEEDS / T: 0113 24 24 333
ROAR/OVER 18 / ID WILL BE REQUIRED

HiFi Club
2 Central Road (0113) 242 7353
Enduring favourite on the Leeds club scene. The sleek modern interior has finally completed the club's image as preferred choice for funked-up soul and Motown lovers. Add cheap drink offers, lager on draught and a friendly crowd, and you'll find a club very close to perfection. 'Move On Up' remains the club's hugely popular trademark, and monthly rock night 'Pigs' is a welcome change of pace. Spot on.
Mon-Wed 10pm-2am, Thu 10pm-2.30am, Fri 10pm-3am, Sat 10pm-3am (comedy night from 7pm), Sun 12pm-12.30am
Mon £4/£3.50, Tue £2.50-£5 (depends on night), Wed £4/£3.40, Thu £5/£4, Fri £6/£5, Sat £6/£5 (comedy £10), Sun free

Jumpin' Jaks
Quebec Street (0113) 242 4333
Sick of spending four hours deciding which 'ironic' pair of stilettos to combine with your day-glo all-in-one before that all important night out? Aren't we all? Well Jumpin' Jaks could be just what you're looking for. This is one of those places where hedonistic pur-suits come before posing and if you don't leave with a stagger in your step and some bloke/bird's phone number in your pocket you must have spent the night asleep in the toilets. Go on, next time someone suggests a night swanking it up around town persuade them to try JJ's instead and let that hair swing loose. Linked to Majestyk at weekends, and on Fridays all drinks are free. Need we say more?
Tue &Thu 9.30pm-2am, Fri-Sat 8.30pm-2am, Sun 9.30pm-1am
Tue £2.50 b4 11pm, £3.50 after, Thu £3 b4 11pm, £4 after, Fri £14 (drinks free all night - £3 off for women, £1 off for men with flyer befor midnight), Sat £6, Sun £2 b4 11pm, £3 after

Majestyk VODKA KICK
City Square (0113) 242 4333
Who says size doesn't matter? When what you're looking for is some sizeable pulling potential, plenty of booze and no snooty types elbowing you out of the way at the bar then Majestyk's your man. Loud, brash and totally unapologetic, it's not everyone's cup of tea, but for sure fire pulling action and boozy fun with your mates there's few places finer to 'ave it. It's linked to Jumping Jaks on weekend nights, with the high point being Saturday's 'Up All Night' where the club is open until 5am, featuring guest DJs starting at 2am, a range of live events and a breakfast club. Wipe yourself out on the Sabbath here.
Tue, Thu & Fri 10pm-2am, Sat 10pm-5am
Tue b4 11pm £2.50, £3.50 after, Thu £3, Fri £14 (drinks free all night - £3 off for women, £1 off for men with flyer before midnight), Sat £6

Mint Club

8 Harrison Street (0113) 244 3168

In the last few years The Mint Club has earned itself a rock-solid reputation for being one of the coolest nightspots in town, with some of the best nights to keep the punters grooving. New Saturday night additions Technique and Asylum are added to a list of already impressive soirees including the legendary Funky Wormhole and new Friday nights, Divided By Dirt and One Love and Resident which keep the punters flocking in. Small and intimate with the coolest mint-themed décor around, super clubs can only dream of their kind of clubber loyalty. It can get very packed (i.e. hot and sweaty), but since when has success ever been a downside?

Mon-Thu 10pm-4am, Fri-Sat 10pm-6am
Call for prices (Call the club not itchy)

Mission

8-13 Heaton's Court 08701 220 114

Leeds' newest clubbing venture is brought to you by the people behind Club Federation and Fibre (you can imagine the carnage). Housed in five railway arches and with a capacity of 1200, nights include student-fests 'I-candi' and 'Vodka Nationwide' and more housey affairs 'Pukka' and 'Funkissential'. Loud manic and completley up-for-it, its adjoining bar Arch 54 is the perfect place to get you in the dancing mood - like most of Leeds clubbers need persuading...

The HiFi Club
2 Central Road, Leeds, Yorkshire, LS1 6DE
Club, Bar, Comedy & Live Music Venue
Playing The Sounds Of Jazz, Funk, Hip Hop, Tamla Motown, Jamaican Ska, Latin, RnB, Electro, Northern & Sixties Soul.
Open Seven Nights A Week & Home To The Funksoulnation, Moveonup, Sunday Joint, Harlem Bush Club, Sweet Revival, Boogaloo, Pigs & Critical Beatdown Clubnights

The HiFi Club 2 Central Road Leeds West Yorkshire United Kingdom. Tel: 0113 242 7353. Web: www.thehificlub.co.uk

MiNT LEEDS

To find out more dates on what's happening at the Mint Club Leeds, check the official Mint Club Web Site at . . .

INFO LINE 0113 244 3168   **AVAILABLE FOR PRIVATE HIRE**

www.**themintclubleeds**.co.uk

Space ~~VK~~ VODKA KICK
Hirsts Yard (0113) 246 1030

Stock trade is DnB, hip hop, and garage of the darker variety in a world of chic glass and brightness. You'll find it packed to bursting at weekends and worth a look in the week for a more low-key vibe. The drinks are pricey, but then they seem to shift more water than anything else – dancing like a maniac is thirsty work.

Mon-Thu 10pm-2am, Fri-Sat 9.30pm-3am/4am.Mon-Thu £3-£5, Fri £5-£7, Sat £7-£10, Sun £5-£8

Rehab ~~VK~~ VODKA KICK
Assembly Street (0113) 223 7647

The clubbing mecca into which Back to Basics was reborn. Dave Beer et al finally manage an entire club instead of one night. The medical-themed interior is a genius touch in the renovated 17th century venue. It's a good marketing ploy, offering rehab for the post-chemical generation. Unfortunately though, the general coup is that Rehab has lost it. The Basics which made Beer legendary falls flat on its face in this new, up-itself venue. A case of complacence maybe - a club can't succeed on reputation alone.

Mon & Wed-Thu 10pm-2.30am,
Fri 10pm-4am, Sat 10pm-4am/6am
(Basics), monthly Sun 10pm-4am
Mon-Thu £3-£5, Fri £8-£10, Sat £10 b4
11pm, £12 after, Sun varies

Bars With DJs

Milo
Revolution
brb
Sandinista
Northern Light

soul and funky grooves keep the dancefloor jiving – which is fair enough as you're gonna need a bit of exercise after spending the first half of the evening in the bar and restaurant.
Fri-Sat 10pm-2.30am
£5-£7
Free membership available
For admission, line-ups and opening times during the week see online listings

Ford**Fiesta**

Think Tank

Call Lane (0113) 234 0980

Think Tank is a fantastic little club with the kind of hidden doorway you don't quite dare negotiate. Still this is part of the point – a seedy venue, indie tunes and a crowd that are happy to hide from the rest of the world as long as no-one tries to mess with the DJ's Charlatans collection.
Wed-Thu 10pm-2am, Fri 10pm-3am,
Sat 10pm-2am. £4-£6

The Wardrobe

6 St Peter's Building's, St Peter's Square,
Lower East Side (0113) 383 8800
www.thewardrobe.co.uk

Normally if your mates said you were off to a bar cum restaurant cum club venue, you'd expect a half-arsed attempt at a disco sell-otaped on the side of a place about as rockin' as a WI meeting. But, oh no, The Wardrobe has always been a bit of a cool customer and its downstairs club leaves you feeling a bit spoilt for choice. The cocktails flow like water, and live bands playing jazz,

Warehouse

19-21 Somers Street (0113) 246 8287

Like a terrier who's lost its owner, it started to look like the Warehouse might curl up and mope into oblivion after surrendering SpeedQueen to Stinky's Peephouse last year. Thankfully though, from November SpeedQueen returns to its spiritual home, bringing back the raucous party atmosphere it's struggled to recreate of late with its new weekend efforts. Its location is still rubbish (but then so was Stinky's) but we haven't forgotten how to walk all that way in our sparkly stillettos, we're party folk damn it. And to experience the SpeedQueen glory days once again, we'll walk miles.
Fri 9pm-3am, Sat 10pm-4am. £8-£15

Win Tickets To NYC with itchy & ISIC

itchy have teamed up with **ISIC** to provide one jammy bastard with two tickets to **New York City**... so good they named it twice.

All you have to do is send us a text with the word **'itchy NYC'** and your answer to the following question (a, b, c) to **81800**

How many different itchy guides do itchy produce?

a. 1, b. 16 c. 160

ISIC is the one and only international form of student ID, costing only £7. It provides its members with access to well over **15,000 discounts** in over **100 countries worldwide** and savings and services in the UK that rivals any other student ID card out there.

If you're not in full time education but under 26 – the International Youth Card gives you all the same fantastic discounts.

For more info and to apply: **www.isiccard.com**

gay

www.itchyleeds.co.uk

highlights

• **Boisterous staff at Blayde's**
• **Gorgeous everything at Velvet**
• **Clubbing perfection at Stinky's**

lowlights

• **Feeling like a moose in Fibre**
• **Jaded old queens in The New Penny**

Pubs/Bars

The Bridge
Bridge End (0113) 244 4734
A relaxed pub atmosphere without the blackened windows and gum-stained carpets of the New Penny. It's like a toned down bar, but mercifully avoids the rampant pretensions of some of the nicer gay joints – naming no names (Fibre). It gets pretty busy at weekends, when the tangerine décor is thankfully screened from view. They also have a decent happy hour, guest DJs, and some truly awful karaoke regulars – you know who you are.
Mon-Wed 12pm-11pm, Thu-Sat 12pm-2am, Sun 1pm-12.30am. No food

Blayde's
3-7 Blayde's Yard, Lower Briggate
(0113) 244 5590
Thankfully, Blayde's offers a bit more than just an unimaginative moniker. It's a funky little place with an extreme policy on bar staff – besides pulling pints, their employees have an entertaining habit of launching into synchronised dance numbers which stop just short of embarrassing. This is a brilliant ploy. A venue where the blokes behind the bar are making bigger twats out of themselves than you can only be a good thing. Expect the usual tranny courtesy in the lavs and an upbeat friendly atmosphere. Depending on the night the clientele can veer wildly from life-partner couples to drooling stalkers. But then we've all been

that lascivious fool at one point in our lives. And sometimes, frankly, we just like the attention.

Mon-Thu 2pm-11pm, Fri-Sat 2pm-1am, Sun 2pm-12.30am. No food

Fibre
168 Lower Briggate 08701 200 888

Fibre looks like a beautiful warm oasis from the outside – not just a little tempting on those rainy Leeds nights. The open glass front expands around an entire corner – no doubt a deliberate ploy to show off the well-dressed crowds who grace the inner sanctum. Don't be surprised to see groups of ugly folk with their noses pressed against the glass in dismay. Eliteism is still alive and well in Leeds. Typical hang-out for gorgeous gay guys, with attractive partners to show off and glam girls with new outfits to show off. Strike a pose, if you can be arsed, otherwise stick with the ugly folk – you'll have more fun.

Mon-Thu 11am-1am, Fri-Sat 10am-2am, Sun 10am-12am
Food: Mon-Sun 12pm-7pm
Sausage and mustard mash £5
House wine: £9.50

Cheap Drinks/Happy Hours

mook – all day sun, mon-thu 5pm-8pm, fri-sat 5pm-9pm (2 4 1 cocktails, £1.80 stella, £7 bottles of wine)

walkabout – mon-thu evenings (2 4 1 bottles)

brb – mon-sun 5pm-8pm & fri-sat 12am-2am (carlsberg £1.80, house wine £6, house spirits doubles for the price of singles)

squares – wed-thu 7pm-11pm (2 for £5 cocktails), thu 7pm-11pm (3 4 2 shooters)

bar pacific – mon-thu 5pm-8pm, fri 5pm-1am (2 4 1 red & stella)

headingley taps – cheap all the time

FordFiesta

The New Penny
57 Call Lane (0113) 243 8055

I've heard that the New Penny claims to be the oldest gay bar in the UK. Claims? Claims? Of course it's the oldest gay joint. You couldn't get any more dated than The New Penny. It's probably featured in a Frankie Howerd sketch. It does look pretty intimidating from the outside, and you can bet there'd be people nailing themselves back inside the closet if they thought this was the only type of gay pub around. Still popular at the weekends though, and you've got to admire the place for tenacity and loyal regulars.

Mon-Tue 12pm-11pm, Wed 12pm-2.30am, Thu-Sat 12pm-2.30am, Sun 2pm-12.30am. No food

Queens Court
167 Lower Briggate (0113) 245 9449

Queens Court offers up the usual deal of scruffy environs at trendy prices. Still, its atmosphere is unsurpassed, with a welcome mix of young and old getting down to diva anthems. The music gets a tad more credible at the weekends and everyone's up for a blinding good time. If you find yourself wondering where all the lovely ladies are, then go to the toilets. They're all in there smoking and having a gossip. I apologise to any hardcore feminists that might get offended by this claim but I'm afraid it is absolute fact.

Mon-Sat 12pm-2am, Sun 12pm-12am
Food: Mon-Sun 12pm-7pm

Velvet
11-12 Hirst's Yard (0113) 242 5079

Understandably hated by great swathes of normal folk. The gorgeous clientele can be depressing to say the least. It's down a posh little alley too, so there's a definite build-up. Get turned away for your dirty trainers and it's the walk of shame back to the tired old town centre. But the atmosphere inside,

once you've braved the gorgon on the door, is nothing short of glorious – it's nice to feel like one of the beautiful people for a while.

Mon-Thu 11am-11pm, Fri-Sat 11am-2am, Sun 12pm-10.30pm
Food: Bar as above, Restaurant from 7pm

Clubs

Stinky's Peephouse
1 Brick Street (0113) 247 0606

The single sex nights have been known to irritate a few people, but generally, Stinky's is a much loved venue. It scores a double whammy by providing one of the best clubs in town with none of the downsides of popular straight places. No queues, cheap entrance, cheap drinks, the best DJs, (but sadly no more SpeedQueen) and all amidst three beautiful floors of high class clubland. And then there's all the gorgeous gay folk of course. It's strictly queer, so no sneaking your straight mates in dressed in lamé tank tops. They'll spot the flabby arms and pasty skin a mile off.

Phone for more details

Buy the books online... www.itchycity.co.uk/books

itchy insider guides 2004

16 to collect

Bath Birmingham Brighton Bristol Cambridge Cardiff Edinburgh Glasgow Leeds Liverpool London Manchester Nottingham Oxford Sheffield York

www.itchycity.co.uk/books

www.itchycity.co.uk

Also well worth a look are **Poptastic** at The Cockpit and the monthly hedo-fest **Federation** at Granary Wharf – see club section of this guide for venue details.

Shops

Clone Zone
164 Briggate (0113) 242 6967
Trendy gay man's shop selling everything from R18 DVDs, to clubwear, magazines, CDs and sex toys. Also stocks rubber and fetish-wear for very naughty boys.
Mon-Thu 11am-7pm, Fri-Sat 12pm-7pm

Other Info

SHOUT free local pink paper
MESMAC advice on men's sexual health (0113) 244 4209
Lesbian & Gay switchboard (0113) 245 3588
Leeds Uni Union LGB leedslgb@mail.com
Leeds Met Uni LGB leedslgb@hotmail.com
Rainbow Weekend annual weekend event in June/July in Hyde Park

shopping

www.itchyleeds.co.uk

highlights

- **Glamourous browsing at Harvey Nic's**
- **Cool kid clobber at Hip**
- **Top secondhand shops in town**
- **Losing hours in Jumbo Records**

lowlights

- **Being too skint to shop**
- **Choice anxiety in Polar Bear**

Shopping Areas

Knightsbridge of the north, my ass. OK we do have a Harvey Nichols but Knightsbridge doesn't have an Everything A Pound shop...

The White Rose Centre
Dewsbury Road, Jnc 28, M62
(0113) 229 1234
Loads of high street brands all under one roof, and it's open late throughout the week. There's nothing too original here, and there's no oxygen to breathe at the weekend, but it can be quite handy.

The Victoria Quarter
Briggate & Vicar Lane (0113) 245 5333
For flashing the cash soap-star style you need to be in this archetectural treat, stuffed full of designer boutiques.

The Corn Exchange
Vicar Lane/Call Lane (0113) 234 0363
Should sort you out for anything from a shiny clubbing outfit to a bonsai tree. Loved by the rrrock kid massive who hang around looking miserable and over eye-lined outside.

Granary Wharf
Canal Basin (0113) 244 6570
Much more than just a place to go shopping, Granary Wharf has cafés and restaurants, street entertainers, an exhibition space and a massive 1000 capacity warehouse space for events. The shops draw the

biggest crowds with everything from Moroccan interiors to Egyptian handicrafts and goth gear and pine furniture.

Mon-Sat 10am-5.30pm, Sun 10am-5pm (times vary between individual venues)

The Light
The Headrow (0113) 218 2060

Bringing together fashion and retail, restaurants, bars, nightclubs, a 13-screen cinema and a health club, The Light is rammed with top shopping, nice restaurants and cool nightlife. Cliché alert, but there's something for everyone here, from drinking in stylish bars, dancing the night away or topping up on retail therapy. Once you're shattered from all that you can always catch a film at Leeds' only city centre cinema, Ster Century. Or for healthy living, you can have a workout or a relaxing beauty treatment at Esporta Health & Fitness Club. No need to risk the hairdo either, as everything you could want is all under one roof, there's also a secure car park where you can leave the car overnight for less than a fiver if you pick it up before 9.30am the next day – which is handy when that quick drink after work turns into an all night session.

Mon-Thu 6am–12.30am, Fri 6am-2.30am, Sat 8am-2.30am, Sun 8am–12.30am
www.thelightleeds.co.uk

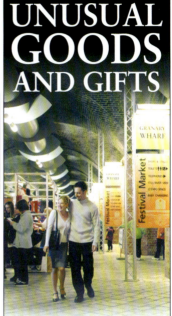

a trip to the **light**...
fantastic!

just found a great place for shopping, eating, drinking, working out and movie watching!

having fun!

wish you were here.

the light
Leeds

Dept. Stores & a Market

Harvey Nichols
107 Briggate (0113) 204 8888

A Leeds shopping institution and walking symbol of desire, Harvey Nics purveys drop-dead gorgeous fashion at drop-dead prices.
Mon-Wed 10am-6pm, Thu-Fri 10am-7pm, Sat 9am-7pm, Sun 11am-5pm

House of Fraser
140-142 Briggate (0113) 243 5235
Pants, jeans, plenty of bling and duvet covers.
Mon-Wed & Fri 9am-5.30pm, Thu 9am-7pm, Sat 9am-6pm, Sun 11am-5pm

TKMaxx
27 Albion Arcade (0113) 246 7990
If Victoria Beckham auctioned off her clobber from the pre-David wilderness years this would be what was left after Emma and Mel C got what they wanted.
Mon–Sat 9am-5.30pm, Sun 11am-5pm

Leeds Kirkgate Market
Vicar Lane (0113) 214 5162
All the cheap 'n' cheerful bananas, broccoli and braising beef a budding Martin Fowler could ask for. And for the history buffs it's where Mr Marks met Mr Spencer.
Mon-Tue & Thu-Sat 9am-5pm, Wed 'til 1pm

Clothing

Unisex

Ace
9 Duncan Street (0113) 245 4555
A regular haunt for Leeds sk8ter bois and the Avril Lavigne army. Cool stuff that's begging to be touched by your sullen angst-ridden mitts.
Mon-Thu 10.30am-5.30pm, Fri-Sat 10am-6pm

Ark
Corn Exchange (0113) 244 4900

Sells the current student uniform (Bench jacket and baggy jeans) at pretty reasonable prices (for Leeds). Also stocks Gold Digga, Custard and Carhaart goods.
Mon-Sat 9am-5.30pm, Sun 11am-4.30pm

Cyberdog
Lower Level, Corn Exchange (0113) 246 7749
You don't come here to browse, your hardcore largin' it radar brings you here like it's a mission from God. PVC, weird spikes and stuff to make your serotonin deficient brain register a smile.
Mon-Sat 9am-5.30pm, Sun 11am-4.30pm

The Dark Angel
Corn Exchange (0113) 245 1112
Dark and mysterious clothes for goths, funeral directors and Milk Tray men.
Mon-Sat 9am-5.30pm, Sun 11am-4.30pm

Diesel
57-59 Vicar Lane (0113) 242 1719
Trendy jeans for those who like a hiked up price tag with their wardrobe basics.
Mon-Sat 9.30am-6pm, Sun 11am-4.30pm

Exit
Corn Exchange (0113) 246 9301
Quality skate clobber for birds and blokes as well as footwear, skateboards, and accessories. All you could need to kit you out for, erm, hanging round outside the Corn Exchange.
Mon-Sat 9.30am–5.30pm,
Sun 11am-4.30pm

Flannels
68 Vicar Lane (0113) 234 9977
Here they specialise in super cool clobber for very 30-somethings. Labels include D&G mainline, YSL Gauche, Gucci, Prada, Evisu and Fake London. It is expensive, but the threads are gorgeous.
Mon-Fri 9.30am-5.30pm, Sat 9am-6pm,
Sun 11am-4.45pm

Great Clothes
84 York Road (0113) 235 0303
Huge clothing store catering for pretty much every member of the family, which specialises in the current season's discounted designer items. Brands sold include FCUK, Firetrap, Gas, Hooch, Kickers and Levi's and include sportswear and clothes for the older generation. A wedding hire facility is also offered as well as a free alteration service meaning that your dad needn't worry too much about his expanding waistline.
Mon-Fri 9.30am-9pm, Sat 9.30am-6pm,
Sun 11am-5pm

Hip
9/14-16 Thornton's Arcade
Men's (0113) 242 4617
Women's (0113) 234 7655
Hip indeed. These two flog funky Stussy, Duffer, Hysteric Glamour and Diesel stuff to the coolest kids in town.
Mon–Sat 10am-5.30pm, Sun 11am–4pm

O'Neill
The Light, The Headrow (0113) 245 5114

O'Neill caters for the more serious surfer (you know the ones that actually own a surfboard and occasionally venture out on the waves). The focus is more on practicality than fashion but they do really funky accessories that mere mortals can purchase without feeling fake.
Mon-Wed & Fri 9am-6pm, Thu & Sat 9am-7pm, Sun 11am-5pm

Strand
153 Briggate (0113) 243 8164

If Posh came to Leeds instead of spending all her time hanging out with gangsta rappers she'd stop by this place for a few choice items. Chloe, Helmut Lang, D&G and everything else a footballer's wife could possibly desire. Totally glam.
Mon-Fri 9.30am-6pm, Sat 9am-6pm, Sun 11.30am-4.30pm

Proibito
The Light, The Headrow (0113) 242 9496

Discount designer wear, now you're talking. Talking crap more like. Some of the stuff you wouldn't mind exchanging a fine English sterling for but the rest should be heading its way towards some huge scissors. If you happen to be in The Light and fancy a game of put together the worst outfit conceivable to mankind; then this is the retail comedian's dream.
Mon 9.30am-5.30pm, Tue-Wed & Fri-Sat 9am-6pm, Thu 9am-7pm, Sun 11am-5pm

Vivienne Westwood
15 County Arcade (0113) 245 6403

The only one in Yorkshire, good old Viv has graced the Leeds massive with her fine designer threads. So much fun to look at, but her crazy designs aren't suited to everyone, bearing in mind she did once dress the Sex Pistols. Shop here for the latest catwalk crazes, just don't come limping towards us when you fall off your eight-inch stilettos and rip your impractically tight linen shirt. Keep telling yourself; it's all the rage in Milan.
Mon–Sat 10am-6pm

Zara
129-132 Briggate (0113) 380 4620

Not the princess with the pierced tongue, but a huge Spanish shop filled with classy clothes. Bliss. Well-made clothing at decent prices and very popular.
Mon-Wed 10am-6pm, Thu-Fri 10am-7pm, Sat 9am-6pm, Sun 11am-5pm

Women's

Accent
18-20 Queen's Arcade (0113) 243 2414

Slick clothes for home girls with style, situated in the Queens Arcade. You'll immediately want everything all at the same time. They stock Miss Sixty, Nolita, Replay, Nas Nas, G Star, Diesel, Firetrap, Free Soul, Sticky Fingers, Tara Jarmon, Gotham Angels and Hunters & Gatherers. This is the kind of shop that makes saving schemes impossible.
Mon–Sat 9.30am-5.30pm, Sun 11am-4pm

Aqua
Corn Exchange (0113) 243 3336

Don't eat for three days prior to visiting this shop - the clothes are so small they'd have a job on to dress Barbie. Thankfully the cash you'll save by starving yourself should help out when you get to the cash desk – these small things don't come cheap.
Mon–Fri 10am–5.30pm,
Sat 10am-5.30pm, Sun 12pm-4pm

Dawn Stretton
30 Central Road (0113) 244 9083

Keeping it real, our Dawn graduated from the Leeds College of Art and Design before setting up shop in the beauty that is the Corn Exchange. Now moved to bigger prem-ises, she specialises in evening wear and has dressed a whole host of beauties including the poor man's Posh, Louise Nurding.
Mon–Sat 9.30am–5.30pm, Sun 11am-5pm

Joseph
78 Vicar Lane (0113) 242 5458

For the more mature amongst us, think Miranda from Sex And The City – sexy, classy but kind of demure. Only the finest tailored clothing is sold here, we're talking pinstripe suits, crisp white shirts – clothes designed for the working woman (business women not hookers in case you're confused).
Mon-Fri 9.30am-5.30pm
Sat 9.30am-6pm, Sun 11am-5pm

Oasis
Commercial Street (0113) 243 2336

Up-to-the-minute girly clothes, fabulous handbags, shoes and sparkly accessories. It's like teasing a small child with a Drumstick lolly – resistance is futile, spend away.
Mon-Fri 9.30am-5.30pm,
Sat 9.30am-6pm, Sun 11am-5pm

Tunnel
22 Queen's Arcade (0113) 243 9996

This tiny independent boutique is filled to the brim with funky clothes – from adventurous garms for the more creative dresser to downright desirable items you'll fight for.
Mon-Thu 9.30am-5pm,
Fri-Sat 9.30am-5.30pm

Vicky Martin
42 Victoria Quarter (0113) 244 1477

Funky clubwear, for those glory days before the pints catch up with your waistline.
Mon-Sat 10am-6pm

Men's

Accent
11-13 Queen's Arcade (0113) 243 1707
Although tucked away in the Queens Arcade, this shop ranks on a par with the big boys over in the Victoria Quarter. Boasting one of the best and most varied range of brands in the city, Accent is a favourite for blokes prepared to part with their hard-earned cash for clobber.
Mon-Sat 9.30am–5.30pm, Sun 11am-4pm

Aspecto
1 Queen Victoria Street (0113) 245 0150
Much like Bertha, Aspecto turns the goods out with a range of fab shoes and smart clobber for men on a mission.
Mon–Sat 9am-6pm, Sun 11.30am–4.30pm

Chimp
5 Thortons Aracde (0113) 234 9979
An essential port of call on a shopping trip out and around town. This funky store, tucked away in the Thorton's Arcade stocks street brands and an in-demand range of trainers. People have been known to travel from miles around to get some new T-shirts here, the regular sales help cut down on your travel expenses.
Mon-Sat 9.30am-5.30pm

Envy
97 Briggate (0113) 245 8045
Mid-price range clothery for the more discerning, but not too flush, man about town. Think more of your 'my interests are fine wine and classic cars' types than 'no, really, check out my ollie'. Still, there's nothing wrong with smart casual and Tim Wheeler from Ash obviously likes it – he wrote a song about it.
Mon-Tue 9am-5.30pm, Wed-Sat 9am-6pm, Sun 11am-5pm

Gieves & Hawkes
98 Briggate (0113) 244 6261
Expensive, but the suits are made to measure so get the plastic out. They sell casual wear too (but nothing you'd go rolling in the hills in), and some smart shoes.
Mon 10am-6pm, Tue–Sat 9.30am-6pm

Secondhand

Blue Rinse
11 Call Lane (0113) 245 1735

If there's one thing we know how to do in Leeds, it's secondhand shopping. Blue Rinse is probably the finest of the city's selection with its leather jackets, jeans, cords and retro t-shirts. It's not as cheap as Oxfam, but then you can't put a price on vintage chic these days darling.
Mon-Fri 10.30am–6pm, Sat 10am-6pm, Sun 11am-4.30pm

The Final Curtain
Headingley Lane (no phone)
We all like to pretend we're at the cutting edge of fashion, but for those who appreciate individual vintage one offs like a true style guru, here's the place to find them. Ball gowns, tuxes, shoes, accessories and casual wear (all original pieces from the 1930s onwards) galore. You'll be hard pressed to find a more friendly shop owner in the whole of Leeds too and that's a fact.
Tue-Sat 11am-5.30pm

Positively 13 O'Clock
7a Crown Street (0113) 243 2776
They're so organised they've even got their own website from which you can purchase vintage goodies. They've got a great selection of stylish pieces from your classic shoes to your cool battered leather jackets. Stuff for both the guys and the gals including accessories, so you can both be the stylish 70s couple that you've always wanted to be. Hey, just like your parents.
Mon-Thu 11am-5.30pm,
Fri-Sat 11am-6pm

ReBop
Corn Exchange (no phone)
Think of a slogan, any slogan. Now walk downstairs in the Corn Exchange to here, and you're bound to find it one of their T-shirts, either new or secondhand. The used ones start from about a fiver, and they sell some of the best flares in Leeds (both new and used) as well as retro shirts and a smattering of jackets.
Mon-Sat 9am-5.30pm, Sun 11am-4pm

Sugar Shack
14 Headingley Lane (0113) 226 1020
Famed for its retro stock as well as a place for the unscrubbed of LS6 to buy their jeans. If you're off to a 70s do, then stop off here to purchase your zany wig, porn star glasses or Village People style policeman's outfit. Truly a Hyde Park institution.
Mon-Sat 10am-6pm

whatever turns you on!

Books

Blackwell's
21 Blenheim Terrace (0113) 243 2446

An undergraduate's paradise. It's an unwritten rule that Blackwell's always stock the book you desperately need because a) you haven't read it and b) the 2000 word essay that goes towards your degree is due in tomorrow. Also there's plenty of stuff for us less academic types too.

Mon & Wed-Sat 9am-5.30pm,
Tue 9.30am-5.30pm

Borders
94-96 Briggate (0113) 242 4400

Stocks a huge range of up-to-the-minute books, music, videos and DVDs. Borders is definitely the pick of the bunch as it opens late and they hold regular evening events where you can mingle with the scholarly massive. It's also the only bookshop I know that sells hot chocolate in what can only be described as a soup bowl. Wicked.

Mon-Sat 9am-9pm, Sun 11am-5pm

Just Books
55 Otley Road (0113) 275 4278

A bit like Christine Hamilton, it knows exactly what it's about and doesn't make any apologies. Sells some bargain reads, and is a sterling choice for picking up the latest celeb biography.

Mon-Sat 9am-5.30pm, Sun 11am-4.30pm

Oxfam Books
9 Otley Road (0113) 274 3818

Cheap as chips for secondhand books – bag that copy of Gary Lineker's Soccer Skills.

Mon-Sat 9.30am-5pm, Sun 11am-3pm

Waterstone's
36-38 Albion Street (0113) 242 0839
93 Albion Street (0113) 244 4588

When it comes to book signings, Waterstone's is the daddy. I would give you some fine examples of literary legends that have graced their presence but I'm still bitter that I spent £80 on a load of books I'll never read again and didn't even get to stroke Richard Madeley's newly coiffed do. But I can't end on a bad note cos their service is top-notch - the staff are ever so friendly and

they do a grand job of not making you feel stupid when you ask them to find a book that was situated right under your nose.

Mon-Fri 8.45am-8pm,
Sat 8.45am-6.30pm, Sun 11am-5pm

WHSmith
3-7 Lands Lane (0113) 242 2505
City Station (0113) 243 3059

Brings back fond memories of early September trips to buy a new jotter, rubber and pencil sharpener, and for the fact they sell everything we could ever need be it Blu-Tack, Tortoise Weekly or a glittery pen for those annual thank you notes.

Mon-Sat 8am-6pm, Sun 11am-5pm; Mon-Sat 6.30am-8.30pm, Sun 7.30am-8.30pm

Music

Choonz World-Wide
100-102 Vicar Lane (0113) 244 9966
Supplying quality dance vinyl to the world (and David Morales don't you know?). These chaps really know what they're on about, and offer a mail order service too.
Mon-Sat 10am-6pm

Crash
The Headrow (0113) 243 6743

A smaller in-store selection than its counterparts, though informed and friendly staff will impart their pearls of wisdom on request. And if you want to shout about your band's gig, the walls of this fine establishment can be home to your promotional material, free of charge.
Mon-Fri 9.30am-6pm, Sat 9am-6pm

HMV
1 Victoria Walk (0113) 245 5548
If you're not into your music before you enter this massive store, then you certainly will be by the time you leave. Masses of quality tunes, DVDs, videos, books, posters and a wide selection of vinyl.
Mon-Sat 9am-6pm, Sun 11am-5pm

Jumbo
Unit 5, St John's Centre, Merrion Street (0113) 245 5570
If Jumbo hasn't got it, then it ain't worth having. Buy your music here and you will live long and prosper.
Mon-Fri 9.30am-5.30pm, Sat 9am-5.30pm

Music Zone
69 Briggate (0113) 245 4811
The revolution may not be televised but Music Zone are bravely battling to bring down the price of CDs across the land. Pulp's Hits for £4, the new Sean Paul for a tenner. God speed you mighty warrior.
Mon-Fri 9am-5.30pm, Sat 9am-6pm
Sun 11am-5pm

Out of Step
7 Crown Street (0113) 245 1730
Record shop at the back of skate shop Wisdom selling music to watch sk8ter bois to.
Mon-Sat 10am-6pm

Play Music
Corn Exchange (0113) 243 2777
These independent record stores are a passionate lot and the guys at Play are no exception. Supplying vinyl to DJs and producers as well as the ordinary punter, they'll even keep the shop open for a bit at closing time if you're still browsing.
Mon-Sat 10.30am-5.30pm

Polar Bear
4-5 Grand Arcade (0113) 243 8231
21a North Ln, Headingley (0113) 307232
Filled with new stuff and secondhand gems, Polar Bear is the kind of shop where you'll lose hours. Online mail order and the option to sell back your least favourite CDs make it a solid choice for music fans.
Mon-Sat 10am-5.30pm/6pm;
Mon-Sat 10am-6pm, Sun 10am-5pm

Rock Shack
Cardigan Road (0113) 230 6363
'The guitar shop in Headingley' as their slogan goes… and fair play to 'em they do it well.
Mon-Fri 10am-6pm, Sat 11am-6pm,
Sun 12pm-5pm

Virgin Megastore
Albion Street (0113) 243 8117
Fantastic sales and everything a CD, vinyl or DVD fan has ever dreamt of. Well worth spending your student loan/family inheritance/nephew's trust fund in.
Mon-8am-6pm, Tue-Wed & Fri-Sat 9am-6pm, Thu 9am-7pm, Sun 11am-5pm

Other Cool Shops

Atticus
4 The Crescent, Hyde Park
(0113) 230 2989
The ideal stomping ground for last minute gifts of the sparkly, fluffy or zany ilk.
Mon-Sat 10.30am-5pm/5.30pm

Azendi
39 Otley Road (0113) 278 6176
The bigger and better Azendi (having just moved 20 metres along the same street to larger premises) boasts as many sparkly and silver things as ever. It's a bit pricey (expect to pay £30+ for a necklace), but you'll not find anywhere better in the vicinity. Get in there.
Mon-Sat 9.30am-5.30pm

Global Tribe
22 Thorntons Arcade (0113) 246 1824
Ethnicy gifts including wooden giraffes.
Mon-Sat 10.30am-5.30pm

JJB
28 The Headrow, (0113) 243 2292
Leeds Shopping Plaza, Albion Street (0113) 244 8868
Kirkstall Retail Park (0113) 230 5474
White Rose Centre (0113) 271 4747
Crown Point Retail Park (0113) 242 2826
Colton Retail Park (0113) 260 0400
Unbeatable for men and women's sports and leisurewear. Call for opening times.
www.jjb.co.uk

Rose & Co
13 Thorntons Arcade (0113) 245 4701
Pure girly heaven. Forget about beauty products hidden away in concrete boxes

that look as appealing as a packet of soda crystals, this is pure pink, sweet smelling goodness. Stacked high on traditional dressers, it's the perfect place for browsing and deciding exactly which concoction it'll be that'll turn you into Cameron Diaz.
Mon-Sat 9am-5.30pm, sun 12pm-4pm

Scoot-A-Bout
Cardigan Road (0113) 278 7078

Independent scooter store on the edge of student country (in between Hyde Park and Burley). They won't take advantage of your mod hairdo and sell you a hairdryer with a lawnmower engine for the price of a family saloon – they offer friendly, impartial advice. They sell accessories as well as the coolest, cheapest mode of transport going.
Mon-Fri 9am-5pm, Sat 9am-5pm

Space NK
63 Vicar Lane (0113) 242 6606
You'd expect some of these beauty products to have been to the moon and back for the price you pay for them in here. 69p Tesco shampoo pretty much does it for me, but if you fancy paying for the posh stuff, then head here. Delicious smelling, labelled stock (with trendy packaging to boot), good for making yourself feel like a goddess.
Mon-Wed 10am-6pm, Thu-Sat 9am-6pm, Sun 12pm-5pm

SCENE NOT HERD.

**Tune in to find out
what's hot & what's not!**

Galaxy 105

entertainment & culture

www.itchyleeds.co.uk

highlights

- **Cool music and comedy at HiFi**
- **Feeling cultured at the Picture House**
- **New bands at Joseph's Well**

lowlights

- **Kids at the Showcase**
- **A losing streak at the cricket ground**
- **New bands at Joseph's Well**

Live Music

Cockpit/Rocket
Swinegate (0113) 244 1573

If it's the old-fashioned, underground vibe you're after, you won't do much better than this dingy, but funky gig-pit in the arches under the train station. Voted Radio 1's Live Music Venue of the Year for 2002, it pulls in all of the up-and-coming UK acts as well as some local talent. Battered leather jacket and noughties mullet are a must.

HiFi
2 Central Road (0113) 242 7353

The king of cool where gig venues are concerned, HiFi is the place to catch a bonafide jazz band or soul sista. Maybe not intended as an out-and-out music venue when it was first conceived (HiFi jumped into the shoes of the sorely missed Underground Club at short notice), the HiFi shares the spoils of the soul-cum-jazz-crooner fraternity with The Wardrobe. Sundays see cracking roast dinners served with a side dish of live music – helped down the hatch with a few of the HiFi's trademark large measure spirits.

Joseph's Well
Chorley Lane (0113) 245 0875
Joseph's Well, in the wake of the likes of the Duchess, is just about the only place that properly supports home grown talent. There are gigs most nights as well as frequent acoustic sessions at the weekend. A big room with a solid sound, you'll find the most barginous gigs Leeds has to offer here.

LMU
Woodhouse Lane (0113) 244 460
For a while after the T&C closed, Leeds Met was Leeds' only remaining venue with the capacity to cope with the bigger touring acts. These days the Met shares the pie with the Cockpit and Leeds Uni so it's less active than it was two or three years ago, but still draws a fair share of the action. The sound's decent enough and there's generally no problems getting hold of rancid ale.
Tickets from Jumbo/Crash Records and LMUSU bars

LUU Refectory
Leeds Uni Campus, Woodhouse Lane
Leeds Uni is coming into its own on the bookings side of things. They've pulled in some quality performers over the past year: The Streets, Feeder and Placebo to name but a few. It is however a bit like watching a gig in a corridor, so if you're knee high to a springer spaniel then you'd better rock up early and grab a decent spot. The bar facilities leave a lot to be desired and the music's so loud that no one will hear your screams.
Tickets from CATS in the student union

The Pack Horse
Woodhouse Lane (0113) 245 3980
Size isn't everything and stage space is a tad limited here, but the lighting rig, projector facilities and acoustics are top-notch for a venue of this size. A handful of loyal promoters drag in acts from around the globe, making the Pack Horse one of the most eclectic, alternative venues around. Prices are pretty cheap, but bear in mind your door fee'll only afford you a couple of centimetres of floor space, so bring your own periscope…

The Royal Park
Royal Park Road (0113) 275 7494
Tiny, studentville gig venue with a dingy but intimate basement. You'll find mainly local talent and the odd act from further afield (Manchester, Sheffield), and the acoustics won't blow you away, but its perfect for keeping your eye on up-and-coming artists. It also has its own rock 'n' roll compere with badged baseball cap and swinging ponytail. Nice.

And also worth a look…

The Vine (The Headrow (0113) 203 1820), **The Primrose** (Meanwood Road (0113) 262 1368) and **The New Roscoe** (Bristol Street (0113) 246 0778) for local music; **The Town Hall** (The Headrow (0113) 246 8120) for occasional big acts or classical offerings. **The Fenton** (pg 60) has irregular performances in the upstairs gig room, as does the gem of a venue, the **Brudenell Social Club** (33 Queens Road). **Dr Wu's** (35 Call Lane (0113) 242 7629) is the place for acoustic and open mic nights, but for a more folkier tone, head down to **The Grove** (pg 56) in the hope of searching out the next Eva Cassidy. **The Wardrobe** offers live funk and jazz, whilst **The Corn Exchange** has pledged an allegiance to local live music. Finally, Granary Wharf's **The Blank Canvas** ((0113) 244 6570), has been known to put on some of Leeds' more established acts.

Theatre

City Varieties

Swan Street (0113) 243 0808

'Cor blimey gov'nor!' This 580 seater old time music hall makes a very valiant attempt at maintaining some turn of the century charm. Nowadays you're more likely to find some very good comedy acts – with recent visits from the likes of Dylan Moran, Rob Brydon and Al Murray, the pub landlord. They also keep the good times rolling with regular return performances from music hall legends 'The Good Old Days'. There's also the occasional pantomime thrown in for good measure, along with the odd magician. Jolly good fun.

Box Office: Mon-Sat 10am-6pm
Doors from 12.30pm-3pm (matinees)
from 7.30pm-8pm (evening)
Tickets: around £9 stalls, £22 boxes

Civic Theatre

Cookridge Street (0113) 214 5315

An impressive Victorian interior and the occasional decent show. The Civic is cheap, doesn't even attempt to compete with the West Yorkshire Playhouse and tends to focus on orchestral numbers rather than actual plays. Make sure you order your drinks before the interval – you'll need 'em and the half time rush to the bar is a shameful testimony to English alcoholism.

Box Office: Mon-Sat 12pm-8pm
Café bar: Mon-Sat 6pm-9pm
Doors from 2pm (matinees), from 7.30pm (evening)
Tickets: £4-£15

Grand Theatre
46 New Briggate (0113) 222 6222

Yet another example of beautiful Victorian architecture that has somehow escaped being turned into a car park. It occasionally attracts big touring shows, but these are interspersed with some right oddities. Still it's good value, and closer to town than the Playhouse if you want to catch last orders.
Box office: Mon-Sat 10am-9pm, Sun 11.30am-7pm
Doors from 2.30pm & 5pm on Sat (matinees), from 7.15pm-8pm (evening)
Tickets: £5-£46

LMU Theatre
Woodhouse Lane (0113) 283 5998

If you like contemporary theatre then LMU certainly delivers. Newcomers should bear in mind that student directors like to 'experiment' with form, genre, and just about everything else. Broadly speaking this means something along the lines of a rap-opera about a lampshade performed by semi-naked writhing girls pretending to be the Indian Ocean. Or something like that.
Box office: Mon-Sat 9.30am-4.30pm
Doors from 7.30pm
Tickets: from £3.50

West Yorkshire Playhouse
Playhouse Square, Quarry Hill (0113) 213 7700

The big one for theatre, live performance, dance and numerous other live acts. You name it, they show it and that's why they call it the West Yorkshire Playhouse, I guess. Inside it becomes more of an arts complex with its own little branded café, restaurant and all manner of other facilities.
Box office: Mon-Sat 9am-8pm
Doors from 1pm (matinees), from 7.30pm (evening). Tickets: £6-£25

Independent Cinemas

Cottage Road Cinema
7 Cottage Road (0113) 275 1606

Cottage Road suffers from not being the Hyde Park Picture House, which is always inundated with student film types. In comparison, this little independent venue seems to have less character and a less artistic selection of films. It's unfortunate really, as were it not for its student nemesis, this would be regarded as the cultural screen showing venue of the city. It manages to keep afloat though and good on it.
Showings: Mon-Sun 6pm-8.30pm
Matinees: Sat 2pm, Sun 3pm
Tickets: Adults £3.80-£4.50, conc £3

Hyde Park Picture House
Corner Brudenell Road (0113) 275 2045

A cool little Victorian cinema with original seating, décor and (probably) odour, which shows cult classics which work well in the antique surroundings. They sensibly forked out for Blair Witch and scared the bejeesus out of many a hapless cinema goer. Rocky Horror Picture specials are also worth a visit: people go in fancy dress and everything.

Showings: 6pm-9pm (matinees Sat 12pm) Adults £3.80, conc £3, OAPs/kids £2.80, Gold Card users £2.50, Friends of Hyde Park £2.80, Sat matinees: kids 20p

Lounge Cinema
North Lane, Headingley (0113) 275 0900

Misleadingly commercial looking cinema in Headingley. They show a limited selection of the best current releases, are licenced to serve alcohol and pack in a crowd most nights.

Showings: 5.20pm-10pm, Tue OAPs 2pm Adults £4.30-£5.30, kids £3.30-£3.80, OAPs £3.30, NUS £3.30

Mainstream Cinema

Showcase
Jnct 27 off M62, Batley (01924) 420 622

Adults £5.25, kids £4.20, NUS £4.20, Tue £3.75. Mon-Sun 10.30am-10pm

Ster Century
The Light, The Headrow 0870 240 3696

Adult £4.50-£5.50, kids £4, NUS £4
Mon-Sun 10am-11pm

Warner Village
Cardigan Fields, Kirkstall Road, 08702 406 020, (0113) 279 9855 (enquiries)

Adult £5.20, kids £3.70, NUS £3.50
Mon-Sun 10am-10pm

Comedy Venues

The Arc
19 Ash Road (0113) 275 2223

Popular Monday night comedy club during term time, expect two top comics compered by Elliot J Huntley, regular drinks deals and a caption competition in the interval which is actually much more fun than it sounds.

Mon 8.30pm-11pm. £4

The Comedy Store
13A Merrion Way

The most famous brand in comedy comes to Leeds. Its clubs in Soho and Manchester are the stuff of legend and hopefully this one will be too. Opens Dec 2003, and should be good for a laugh.
www.thecomedystore.co.uk

HiFi Club
2 Central Road (0113) 242 7353

An independent Saturday night comedy club standing in staunch opposition to the establishment. HiFi offers early evening comedy, with the show finished by 10pm but the ticket price lets you into their normal club night too where you can do your own comedy moves 'til 3am. The stand-up is terrific, with their recent alumni including Ross Noble, Reginald D Hunter and Brendon Burns – all grand masters of their art. There's always plenty of rolling around on the floor, if not at the gags then as a result of their super large spirit measures.

Sat 7pm-10pm, with club night till 3am
£10/£9 (members) – £4 refund if you don't
stay for the club

Jongleurs
The Cube, Albion Street 0870 787 0707

The McDonalds of the comedy scene, it's corporate, it's mainstream and, unlike Micky D's, it's very expensive (£8-12 door tax, and super pricey food and drink). Good for hen and stag do's, but you won't see much original new comedy in here. The cheesy disco later is good for a laugh tho'.

Thu-Sat 7pm-11pm (show starts 8.30pm,
disco 'til 2am). £8 Thu, £12 Fri-Sat

Hyena Lounge
Upstairs at The Original Oak, 2 Otley
Road, Headingley (0113) 275 1322

Absolutely cracking Thursday night comedy club, The Hyena Lounge, in the upstairs room of The Original Oak, is exactly what live comedy should be all about. Everyone crams into a small room, there's a great bond between the audience and the comics and you always laugh your tits off – it's for these reasons that the Hyena is rated by most comedians as the best room to play in the North. Hence loads of top circuit acts make the trip out of London to play here. It's always rammed so get there early.

Thu doors 8pm, show 9pm. £5

Abbey House Museum
Kirkstall Road (0113) 230 5492

Museum specialising in recreating Victorian life. If you've an interest in this period it's well worth a visit, and even sworn anti-history types might be converted. Witness the crazy and time consuming ways people used to fill up their time before TV. These range from scraping sugar off huge white pillars to selling material by the ream. Be thankful those days have passed.

Tue-Fri 10am-5pm, Sat 12pm-5pm,
Sun 10am-5pm (last admission 4pm)
Adults £3, conc £2, kids £1

the itch

Celebrity Spotting Leeds Style....

You may not see as many faces down Briggate as down Chelsea way, but don't be fooled into thinking that Leeds is as barren of screen talent as a roomful of budgerigars...

Yorkshire Television – Home to Calendar (Harry and Christa eat your heart out), Emmerdale's indoor bits and the legendary Countdown.

Programmes filmed in & about Leeds – Contrary to popular belief some of the scenes from A Clockwork Orange were not filmed in the Roger Steven's building at Leeds Uni, so stop saying they were. 'Filmed in Leeds' claims we can include are Fat Friends (Weight Watchers meetings filmed inside that village hall opposite Tariqs in Headingley), Touch Of Frost (some office scenes are filmed in a redundant building in Headingley Office Park on Otley Road), Heartbeat (in the Dales) and of course that nail-biting saga of country folk, Emmerdale.

Famous University Alumni - Barry Cryer, Jack Straw (banned from Leeds Uni Union), Mark Knopfler, Marc Almond (Soft Cell), Nicholas Witchell, Alan Yentob, Nick Owen, and erm, Harold Shipman.

Famous inhabitants past and present (by no means an invitation for stalking) – Leeds' footballers, Emmerdale stars, Kay Mellor, Chumbawumba, Alan Bennet, Angela Griffin, Nell McAndrew, Mel B (Spice Girls, remember?) and our personal favourite, the late Shirley Crabtree (Big Daddy to his mates).

Leeds Industrial Museum
Armely Mills, Canal Rd (0113) 263 7861

Ever wondered why the Leeds crest includes two tortured sheep? If so, this could be the kind of worthy and umm, kind of dull, local history lesson to tempt you...

Tue-Sat 10am-5pm, Sun 1pm-5pm
Adults £2, conc £1

Thackray Medical Museum
Next to Jimmys Hospital (0113) 245 7084

A bit like the only part of the Millennium Dome that was any good. Most people can manage to feign enthusiasm for a while if there's an interactive exhibit or two on offer. Thackray goes all out to make medical matters interesting.

Mon-Sun 10am-5pm
Adults £4.90, conc £3.90, kids £3.50

Tropical World
**Princes Avenue, Roundhay Park
(0113) 266 1850**

Kids seem to love it but then I guess if you're five years old maybe a koi karp and an insect-free insect house seems like a proper day out.

Adults £3, 8-15yrs £2

Art Galleries

Craft Centre
The City Art Gallery (0113) 247 8241

Unlike the rest of the City Art Gallery, these artists actually hope to sell their work. On this basis the bi-annual exhibitions display some interesting original art work For the same reason it's not particularly avant–garde, but that's the price of capitalism.

Mon-Fri 10am-5pm, Sat 10am-4pm. Free

City Art Gallery
The Headrow (0113) 247 8248

Main public art gallery supplying the sensible landscapes and portraits expected of a mainstream gallery. They do also host some excellent contemporary exhibitions and run a picture-lending scheme, which could have you looking cultured and tasteful at a knock down price.

Mon-Tue & Thu-Sat 10am-5pm, Wed 10am-8pm. Free

Henry Moore Institute
74 The Headrow (0113) 234 3158

As a general rule of thumb, if it's interesting, contemporary, and on a grand scale, blame it on Henry Moore. The emphasis is on sculpture here (duh), and you can expect to see the country's finest, expertly exhibited, here – for free!

Mon-Tue & Thu-Sun 10am-5.30pm, Wed 10am-9pm. Free

Yorkshire Sculpture Park
Bretton Hall, Wakefield (0113) 830 579

Not everyone's cup of tea, an art gallery which involves hiking around miles of parkland. If you can handle the whole walking aspect you'll find some of Henry Moore's best work here. Checking out these makes contending with all the nauseating student couples enjoying the fact they're cultured just about bearable.

Grounds, centre & shop – Summer: Mon-Sun 10am-6pm, Winter Mon-Sun 10am-5pm; Galleries – Summer: Mon-Sun 10am-5pm, Winter Mon-Sun 11am-4pm

Headingley Cricket Ground
St Michael's Lane (0113) 278 7394

Spend millions of pounds on renovating your ageing stadium, turn it into a formidable multi-tiered fortress, upgrade the existing stadia and add a dash of nostalgia with some impressive iron gates emblazoned with the names of past Headingley greats and then... get relegated to Division 2. Don't let the club's recent misfortune deter you from enjoying a boozy summer's day on the terrace.

Adults £10-£14, juniors £5-£9

Leeds United
Elland Road (0113) 367 1166

Under the watchful guidance of El Tel, the mighty Leeds fell hard last season, but what more can you expect under the guise of a perma-tanned Southerner? Very narrowly missing the relegation spot in 2003 put the fear of God into the Leeds faithful, with their hatred of a certain Mancunian squad growing by the day. New management staff, the loss of Peter Rid-sale and a freshly shuffled squad for 2004 might not bring back the magical atmosphere at Elland Road there once was, but as Yazz once said – the only way is up.

Adults £19-£35

Leeds Rhinos RLFC
St Michael's Lane (0113) 278 6181

Headingley Rugby Ground – the setting for some of the best homegrown entertainment in Leeds: breathtaking, mesmerising and at times down right outrageous – but enough about Ronnie the Rhino. The mascot is pretty much all the fans have to keep them cheerful these days as the rest of the boneheads on the pitch continue to snatch defeat from the jaws of victory season after season. Always a hive of activity in the summer though, and no citizen of Leeds' Tour of Duty is complete until they've experienced the infamous south stand on a balmy summers eve.
Adults £11-£17

Leeds Tykes RUFC
St Michael's Lane (0113) 278 6181
Sharing the nest at Headingley is rugby union side the Leeds Tykes. Until recently they enjoyed modest success, ever in the shadow of their rugby league co-habitees. Since promotion to the Zurich Premiership though, the Tykes have proved their mettle and over the past couple of seasons have enjoyed ever growing success in the top flight. Punters at Headingley can now watch them mix it up with the likes of the Bath Rahrahs and the Gloucester Henrys. They play with an egg-shaped ball, but it's not real rugby is it, if we're being totally honest...?
Adults from £10

National Martial Arts College
First Floor, 3 Stanningley Road, Armley (0113) 231 0101
The name conjures up images of scores of super-cool ninjas decked out in black, routinely kicking the crap out of a never ending stream of crazy, bandana-adorned Bruce Lee wannabes in the grounds of a grand Oriental palace under the watchful eye of a wise Mr Miagi type character. Sadly, it's not as cool as that, what with it being in Armley and all, but it does live up to the promotional garb of 'Centre of Excellence and Home of Champions' and kickboxing is the house speciality… but I could still have any of 'em.
Mon-Fri 12pm-8pm, Sat 10am-2pm
Membership from £45 a month (includes uniform & insurance)

Yorkshire Dance
St Peter's Building (0113) 243 8765
The Russians have the kosack, the Spanish the flamenco. If Yorkshire had a dance of its own, it'd involve swilling a pint of Tetley's to and fro in front of the football while shouting 'Leeds! Leeds! Leeds!'. Thankfully they don't teach you the ins and outs of that dazzling composition, but you could learn some more credible forms of groove – street, jazz, tap and ballet are just a few of the jigs that you could be mastering here. Jangle that spangle, girlfriend.
(Term time only) Mon-Thu 9am-9pm/9.30pm, Sat 9am-4pm
Adults £4, concs £3

Tourist Attractions

Harewood House
Harewood (at the junction of the A61/A659 on the Leeds/Harrogate Road) (0113) 218 1010

Properly grand stately home on the outskirts of Leeds. Built in the late 1700s, it also provides a home to some 18th century and Italian Renaissance masterpieces, porcelain and Chippendale furniture. But enough of the historical artefacts – the adventure playground (opened by none other than Jack Charlton and Tony Dorigo), café, bird gardens and lake are quite enough to keep the more simple minded culturalists happy.

Mar-Nov: Gardens & playground 10am-6pm, bird gardens 10am-5pm, house & gallery 11am-4.30pm. Freedom ticket (all attractions): Adults £9.50, kids £5.25. Sun & bank hols: Adults £10.50, kids £5.75

Kirkstall Abbey
Kirkstall Road

If the monks who in-habit-ed (ho ho) this 12th century abbey could see the folks gathered in its grounds today, knocking back four-packs of lager in the sunshine, they'd turn in their graves – everyone knows Monks prefer wine.

Lager louts (students) and dog shit aside, the Abbey, located on a lush flood plain on the banks of the River Aire, is a major tourist attraction for the city. Restoration work is under way as we write – until then it just looks like a knackered old church.

24hr access. Free

Meanwood Valley Urban Farm
Sugarwell Road, off Meanwood Road (0113) 262 9759

Conjures up images of blokes in suits running around with their briefcases tucking into bails of straw, but in reality is just a working farm in the middle of an urban metropolis (well, Meanwood) where you can coo over animals and watch farm practises taking place at close quarters.

Mon-Sun 10am-4pm
Adults £1, 12-17 yrs 50p, under 12s free

Roundhay Park
(0113) 266 1850

As much parkland as you could quite honestly ever need and all within an easy bus ride of the city centre. Post-park drinks at the Roundhay Fox pub will ease your tired legs and any remaining troubled minds.

24 hr access. Free

Royal Armouries
Armouries Drive (0113) 220 1999
Holding the national collection of arms and armour in five special galleries covering war, tournament, self-defence, hunting and the armour of the Orient. The exhibits span 3000 years ranging from the primitive to the downright scary. Live demonstrations add a bit of action; try and catch the jousting or fencing if you can. As an added bonus, entry's free and there's a shop should you feel the need to purchase a plastic shield to protect yourself on the mean streets of Leeds. Check itchyleeds.co.uk for details of exhibitions.
Mon-Sun 10am-5pm. Free

Temple Newsham
Off Selby Road (0113) 264 7321
Probably best known as the venue for many a rock concert (this is where the riotous 2002 Leeds Festival was held), it's also worth visiting for its collection of Chippendales (the furniture, not the greasy strippers), fine art and formal gardens. You'll find it five miles out of the city centre and boasting its own restaurant and gift shop if all of that culture starts to take its toll.
House closed until late Autumn 2003, grounds open all year. Farm: Tue-Sun 10am-4pm, Adults £3, kids £2, parking £1.50

Harrogate
A respectable Victorian Spa town full of retired folks and antique lovers. Browse the shops pretending you could flash the plastic if you saw something nice, or wander around the Mercer Art Gallery (01423 556188). A cup of tea and a scone at Betty's Tea Rooms is a must (1 Parliament Street (01423 502746), or take a trip to the Turkish Baths (01423 556746) to wind down after a hard day's shopping. For plant lovers, the bi-annual flower shows are not to be missed.
Trains from £4.70 adult,
£3.10 young persons, £2.35 kids

Ilkley
Spa town in the heart of the Yorkshire moors. Have some pie in one of the pubs, then take a trip to Ilkley Moor to see the Cow and Calf (stones that look nothing like cattle), or some of the prehistoric rock carvings left by the original inhabitants of the moors (a dodgy swastika if you ask me). Whatever you do, don't mention the words 'On Ilkla Moor baht'at', it may well be Yorkshire's anthem but the locals really have heard it all before.
Train fares from £2.80 adults, £1.85 young persons railcard, £1.40 children

Lightwater Valley
North Stainley, Ripon (01765) 635 321
Enough rides for the grown ups to warrant a day out, the highlights being the mile long roller coaster stretching deep into the surrounding forest, and the dark and dingy underground thrill seeker, the Sewer Rat. Plenty for the midgets too with slow, dull rotating things, the 'hilarious' park mascots

and the arbitrary pedal boats. Call ahead for opening times before you get over-excited and arrive to find it closed..

Late Apr-early Nov weekends, half terms & holidays, every day Jul-Aug. Adults £13.50, under 1.2m £12, under 1m free

National Museum of Photography, Film & Television
Bradford (01274) 202 030

Right in the heart of Bradford city centre, this place is one of the most visited national museums outside of London. There's tons here to keep even the most cabbage-brained visitor occupied – check out the old Playschool toys, the IMAX cinema or fiddle with interactive stuff to your heart's content.
Tue-Sun 10am-6pm
IMAX: adult £5, child £4.20

Salts Mill
Victoria Road, Saltaire (01274) 531163

Four miles north of Bradford, its main attraction is the collection of art by Bradford born artist David Hockney. Titus Salt's phenominal mill buildings now house high-tech electronic companies as well as the exhibition stuff, so you'd better have your wits about or you might end up gazing at circuit boards – and that's no fun, not even if you work there.
Mon-Fri 10am-5.30pm,
Sat-Sun 10am-6pm. Free

NationalExpress
easily the best value

Go by coach... to York

Cost: £4.50 day return, £6 return
Time Taken: from 55 mins
Services per day: 4

www.nationalexpress.com

So, sum it up then...
Picturesque, tourists galore, plenty of history and proper boozers

Eating out
Try Meltons Too (25 Walmgate (01904) 629 222) for classy tapas at fine prices or Fiesta Mehicana (14 Clifford Street (01904) 610 243) for the restaurant equivalent of a month on Prozac. Fantastic.

Slake that thirst in style
Hang out on the roof terrace at Kennedy's (1 Little Stonegate (01904) 620 222) or down your own body weight in flavoured vodkas at Rumours (94 Micklegate (01904) 622 225).

Not ready for bed yet
York's not exactly the clubbing capital of the north – try The Gallery (12 Clifford Street (01904) 647 947) or our favourite, The Willow (37 Coney Street (01904) 654 728) – once you've got over the Chinese restaurant vibe you'll have a great time.

What about daylight hours?
Wander round town and soak in the history, browse the shops, hang out by the river.

And when the party's over...
The York Backpackers (88-90 Micklegate (01904) 627 720) is perfect for a flying visit and very cheap.

York

York is the American tourist's dream (and you'll encounter quite a few), what with its age-old crooked buildings and narrow, cobbled streets. Essential visits include the Jorvik Museum, the Minster (of course) and at least one of the historic pubs within the city walls – The Maltings or the King's Arms are good

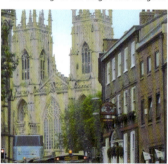

bets. Also home to a number of fine cafes and restaurants – pick up a copy of itchy York 2004 and make your selection wisely.
Trains from £7.60 adults,
£5 young persons, £3.80 children

Yorkshire Dales

You could recreate a trip over the Dales Emmerdale stylee with a tea tray, some bits of gravel and some stalks of broccoli, but it's far more exhilarating to actually feel the rain on your face and smell that pungent country air with your own nostrils. Highlights include Brimham Rocks just outside Ripon, Haworth ('Bronte Country'), and Old Mother Shipton's Cave & Petrifying Well in Knaresborough (she predicted the Fire of London don't you know).

Should the pub landlords stage a strike (it could happen you know – pulling pints is heavy work), some alternatives:

Snooker/Pool

Citrus
11 North Lane (0113) 274 9002
Wed-Sun 9am-4pm & 5.30pm-10pm
Pool: £6/hr

The Elbow Room
64 Call Lane (0113) 245 7011
There's enough here to keep pretty much everyone happy, what with 15 SAM K American pool tables, arcade machines, DJs, food and free flowing beer. The pool is charged by the minute, giving it that added hint of pressure that'll sort the men out from the boys. Decent menu offers take the edge off losing for the 11th time.
Mon-Sat 12pm-2am, Sun 2pm-10.30pm
£5p/hr b4 7pm, £8 p/hr after

Northern Snooker Centre
Kirkstall Road (0113) 243 3015
You'll never be a pool shark if it takes you an hour to get a game on the lone table at your

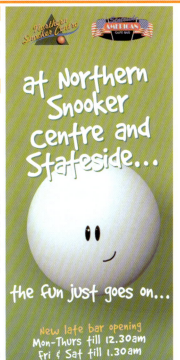

Paintball Commando
Castle Farm, Milthorpe Lane, Wakefield
0808 108 9831
Mon-Sun 9.30am-4.30pm
£15 per day - includes BBQ lunch, 50 balls
and equipment

F1 Racing
Pepsi Max Raceway, Kathryn Avenue
Huntington, York (01904) 673 555
Mon-Sun 11am-7pm
£8.50-£35 per driver

Kart Skill Leeds
South Accomodation Road, Hunslet
(0113) 249 1000
Mon-Fri 10am-10pm, Sat-Sun 10am-5pm
£25 per driver, 1 hour race event

local pub. Here they have 27 full-sized
snooker tables, 21 American Pool tables as
well as food and satellite TV for when you
need rest. It's open almost 24hrs a day and
they hold regular competitions meaning
you've got no excuses for being the worst
player in this side of Halifax.
Mon-Sun 9.30am-7pm
Membership: £6 (conc. £3), £1 for the day
Snooker £4.44p/hr, Pool £5.22p/hr

Casinos

Casinos are still bound by the 24 hour
rule which means you have to join 24
hours before you can go and spunk your
granny's inheritance - entrance and membership is free.

Riley's Pool & Snooker Club
1 Cross Belgrave St (0113) 243 3391
24hr, members only
NUS £3p/hr, members £6p/hr

Gala Casino
Wellington Bridge Street (0113) 389 3700
Sun-Fri 2pm-6am, Sat 6pm-4am

Grosvenor Casino
Merrion Way (0113) 244 8386
Moortown Corner (0113) 269 5051
Sun-Fri 2pm-6am, Sat 2pm-4am

AMF Bowling
Merrion Centre (0113) 245 1781
Adults: £2.70 day, £3.60 eve & w/e

Napoleon Casino
Bingley Street (0113) 244 5393
Sun-Fri 2pm-5am, Sat 2pm-4am

Hollywood Bowl
Cardigan Fields (0113) 279 9111
Sun-Thu 10am-11pm, Fri-Sat 10am-12am
Mon-Fri b4 6pm: Adults £2.60, kids £1.80
After 6pm & w/e: Adults £3.85, kids £2.85

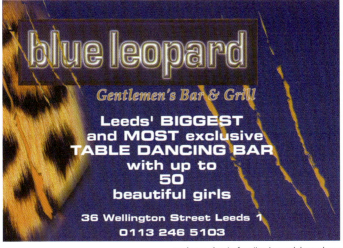

blue leopard

Gentlemen's Bar & Grill

Leeds' BIGGEST and MOST exclusive TABLE DANCING BAR with up to 50 beautiful girls

36 Wellington Street Leeds 1
0113 246 5103

Table Dancing Clubs

Blue Leopard
36 Wellington Street (0113) 245 5103
Leeds' premier club, for very good reasons: over 100 dancers, plush surroundings, open til it gets light (almost). Jo Guest and Jackie Degg are regulars and the 300 capacity venue is usually pretty busy with birthdays and stag dos. In fact I've just celebrated my fourth birthday of the year...
Mon-Thu 7pm-2am, Fri-Sat 7pm-4am
£10 entry, £10 dance

DV8
9 Lower Briggate (0113) 243 4293
Probably the seediest of the seed pits
Mon-Sat 5pm-2am
£10 entry, £10 dance

The Purple Door
5 York Place (0113) 245 0556
Charge up your purple dollars
Mon-Thu 8pm-2am, Fri-Sat 6pm-2am
Mon-Thu £5, Fri-Sat £7 entry, £10 (buy your purple $ at the door) dance

living

www.itchyleeds.co.uk

Property Developers

Barratt Homes
14 Royds Hall Road (0113) 279 0099
www.barratthomes.co.uk

Bryant Homes
3300 Century Way (0113) 232 1400

As one of the country's largest house builders, Bryant Homes have a reputation for admirable commercial and residential developments. Their Aspect 14 development looks to be no exception, located near the Halifax Building, it offers modern and versatile luxury 2 bed apartments boasting panoramic views of the city's skyline.
www.bryanthomes.co.uk

City Walls
**Agents: Hunters, 15 Park Place
(0113) 218 2446**
Launching in 2004, City Walls on Concord Street. 5 minutes from the city centre, offer Leeds city slickers the height of contemporary living. With 171 gorgeously trendy 1 and 2 bed apartments with undercrofted car parking available, interested parties should contact Hunters Estate Agents on (0113) 218 2446
www.citywallcorporation.co.uk

Cala Homes
Victoria House (0113) 239 9500
www.cala.co.uk

Aspect 14 is a brand new Bryant Homes' development of **luxury** 2 bedroom apartments in **Leeds city centre,** next to the Halifax building. Forming two sides of a triangle, the development has at its centre a private landscaped area with **plenty of space** to relax and enjoy the fresh air. The diverse range of **modern** and versatile apartments are designed to suit your own individual lifestyle, as well as giving **panoramic views** over both the city skyline and beyond. Prices start from only **£121,800** for 2 bedroom apartments and there is **no stamp duty*** to pay. Parking is available to selected plots. For more information visit our **show apartments** open daily from 9.30am to 5.00pm (customer car park accessed from Clay Pit Lane), visit our website at **www.bryant.co.uk** or call 0113 245 2889

*On apartments under £160,000

Elevate your lifestyle

Prices from £99,950.

CONCORD

First Class apartments for high flyers.
Five minutes walk North East from Leeds City Centre.
For completion 2004.

For a brochure, please register your details,
call Hunters on 0113 218 2446 or text cityc to 83118.

The development of 171 apartments on both sides of Concord Street comprises studios,
1 Bed, 2 Bed, live work and duplex apartments together with a number of exclusive
Penthouse Suites. Undercrofted car parking is designed to minimise the impact of cars.

A development by:
City Wall Corporation
www.citywallcorporation.co.uk

HUNTERS
city living

www.huntersnet.co.uk

Crosby Homes
Mortec Park, York Road (0113) 265 2000
www.crosbyhomes.co.uk

KW Linfoot
Lancaster House (01904) 690741
www.kwlinfootplc.com

Persimmon Homes
3 Hepton Court (0113) 240 9726
www.persimmonhomes.com

Redrow Homes
Brunel Road, Wakefield (01924) 822566
www.redrow.co.uk

Letting Agents

Headingley Lets
83 Otley Road (0113) 225 1616
Leeds Bridge House (0113) 2251313
Specialising in the lettings market they cover student and professional lets, with properties ranging from small studio flats in the north, west and south suburbs of Leeds to large penthouses in the city centre.
www.headingley.uk.net

Jump
Hepton Court, York Road 08708 446655
In addition to their successful sales service, Jump also offer a lettings side to their business. With properties available across the city, prospective tenants will be helped by expert advisors, and made of suitable properties by sms text alerts, whilst Jump also offer a range of additional products such as

insurance and a range of management services available for landlords.
www.jumpnow.co.uk

LS1
2 Cherry Tree Walk (0113) 234 4111
Fax (0113) 234 4114
A large range of sumptutious pads are available to rent, but they let them quickly so check their website for the latest details.
www.ls-1.co.uk

Manning Stainton
28 Otley Road (0113) 217 9090
With a dozen offices accross districts in the city, MS offers a range of services for landlords and tenants.
www.manningstainton.co.uk

Morgans City Living
32 Park Place (0113) 398 0099
46 The Calls (0113) 398 0098
28 Otley Road (0113) 217 9090

Morgans are well known for managing some extremely flash pads accross the city centre and also in key areas on the outskirks. Not only are the pads gorgeous, they offer a high level of professionalism and in many cases the properties are far more reasonably priced than you would expect to pay.
www.cityliving.co.uk

Residential Sales

Alan Cooke
382 Harrogate Road (0113) 288 8666
www.alan-cooke.co.uk

Carter Jonas
8 Park Place (0113) 242 5155
www.carterjonas.co.uk

Castlehill
21 Otley Road (0113) 278 7427
www.castlehill.co.uk

Hendys
116 Harrogate Road (0113) 268 2100
www.hendersonjones.co.uk

Hunters
15 Park Place (0113) 386 8403
www.huntersnet.co.uk

Jump
Hepton Court, York Road 08708 446655
With offices in Armley, Beeston, Bramley, Chapel Allerton, Garforth, Harehills and Pudsey, Jump have quickly established themselves as a force to be reckoned with in

Join hundreds of people who are already

Jumping

Call us now to see how we can get you moving

Armley	0113 290 7900	Garforth	0113 286 8838
Pudsey	0113 236 3259	Harehills	0113 240 9766
Bramley	0113 236 2684	North Leeds	0113 266 7662
Chapel Allerton	0113 268 7790	South Leeds	0113 387 2500

moving made simple™

www.jumpnow.co.uk

residential sales. With their unique seller scheme they make selling your house as easy as possible with no legal fees, an in-branch mortgage advisor and no advertising fees. For buyers they can advance your deposit, legal fees and survey fees to reduce expensive up-front costs, whilst alerting you to suitable properties by sms text message. *www.jumpnow.co.uk*

LS1

2 Cherry Tree Walk (0113) 234 4111
Fax (0113) 234 4114

LS1 set out to break the mould of estate agency with their motto of being 'Life Agents not Estate Agents' and have established themselves as specialists in dealing with city centre apartments. They're well known for the sale of gorgeous contemporary pads, and offering levels of service that exceed customer expectations. If you don't already know them from their super chic offices on Cherry Tree Walk, then you'll probably have raced their brand new nippy LS1 branded Mini Cooper around the town. *www.ls-1.co.uk*

Pickerings

16 St Annes Road (0113) 274 6746
www.pickeringshomes.co.uk

Funishings and Interiors

Ambienti Design
92 Harrogate Road
(0113) 262 0101

Cave
83 Kirkgate (0113) 244 4901

Domane Interiors
5 Bridge Street (0113) 245 0701

Futon Company
30-32 Woodhouse Lane
(0113) 245 0770

Indonique
81 King Lane (0113) 266 0666

Loft
24-28 Dock Street (0113) 305 1515

Peter Maturi
Vicar Lane (0113) 245 3887

Portafino
80 North Street (0113) 243 8700

Robert Mason
70 North Street (0113) 242 2434

West Park Interiors
20 Swinegate (0113) 245 4522

sexy, desirable pads, not frumpy flats.

Life's too short to spend it with a flat you don't fancy.
Which is why frumpy flats don't get on our books.

city apartments **life agents, not estate agents**

t 0113 2344111 e contact@ls-1.co.uk www.ls-1.co.uk LS1 2 cherry tree walk, the calls, leeds LS2 7EB

body

www.itchyleeds.co.uk

Hairdressers

Box Creative Hairdressing
3 Lower Briggate (0113) 245 6869
In these hip and trendy times, your boring old ponytail just isn't going to cut the mustard. Thank heavens for the folk at Box who know just how to transform your barnet into today's trendiest styles. As well as cutting-edge cuts they offer colouring, conditioning treatments and complete restyles as well as catering for those who fancy a less radical do. The location is dead handy and the staff are well-trained, friendly and they listen. Phew.

Mon-Sat 10am-6/7pm
Women £27.50, men £17.50, NUS 50% off Mon-Wed

Expo
Crown Street (0113) 234 7235
Stylish city centre salon offering equally stylish haircuts, ranging from the more traditional to various contemporary cuts. Masters at colouring services like highlights and naturalisation and always busy, it's advisable to book an appointment in this well-respected hairdressers.
Mon-Sat 8.30am-5pm/6pm (Thu 'til 7pm)
Women from £30, Men £27, NUS 15% discount Mon-Fri

Jam
77 Otley Road (0113) 278 6275
Mon, Wed/Sat 9.30am-5pm,
Tue/Fri 9.30am-6pm, Thu 9.30am-8pm
Women/men £18-£27, NUS 10% off Mon-Tue

Modern Hairdressing
23 Thorntons Arcade (0113) 245 4689
Mon-Wed 9am-6pm, Thu 9am-8pm,
Fri 9am-6.30pm, Sat 8.30am-5pm
Women £25, men £17, no NUS discount

Oasis
37 Otley Road (0113) 278 9214
Mon-Tue 9.30am-5pm, Wed/Sat 9am-5pm,
Thu-Fri 9am-6pm
Women from £21.90, men from £11,
NUS 15% off

Toni & Guy
Boar Lane (0113) 234 4334
22 King Edward Street (0113) 244 9610
Mon-Tue 9am-5.15pm, Wed-Thu 9am-
6.45pm, Fri 9am-6pm, Sat 9am-5pm
Women from £33, men from £26, NUS 10% off
Mon-Wed

XS Hair and Beauty
1 White Cloth Hall (0113) 245 9503

Impressive salon behind the Corn Exchange,
with dedicated stylists and colour techni-
cians to help coiffeur you into the very latest
trends. They also do manicures, pedicures
and nail acrylics using creative products
from Monday to Wednesday.
Mon-Sat 9am-5pm. Women £32, Men £28

Beauty Salons

Nailed On
Corn Exchange (0113) 245 0655
Headrow Centre (0113) 244 8763
Trendy chain, offering everything from mani-

Unit 2
White Cloth Hall
Crown Street
Leeds LS2 7DA
0113 234 7235

EXPO hair design

cures and nail art, to body art and tooth gems
all from fully qualified and experienced tech-
nicians. For those in a hurry, they also offer nail
enhancements in 40 minutes and airbrush
tanning in 20, and their no appointment
needed policy is perfect for girls with hectic
schedules. For a proper beauty sesh, bring a
friend and you'll both get £10 off French
acrylic nails. They also offer products including bindhis, body rocks and piercing jewellery.
Mon-Sat 9.30am-5.30pm, Sun 12pm-4pm
Natural nail enhancement £39

xs hair & beauty

0113 245 9503
1 white cloth hall leeds

Handstanned
Grand Arcade (0113) 246 0030
Mon-Wed/Fri 10am-6pm, Thu 10am-7pm,
Sat 10am-5pm
Full manicure £23, full pedicure £23

Health

Astanga Yoga
Roundhay 07855 443 384
Whether you're already a fanatic or hoping
to embark on the path of yoga, classes don't
come more highly recommended than
these. Suitable for all ages and fitness levels,
and tailored to the individual, you'll find
beginners and improvers classes on offer.
There's also the option of group classes of
individual tuition. Relaxing, energising and
downright good for you.
Yoga at work: 45 minute class available
throughout the day. Beginners, improvers,
relaxing or energising. £6 pp. Min 5- Max 20
per class. Classes in Roundhay: Mon 8pm-
9pm, Tue 7.30pm-8.30pm, Fri 6.15pm-
7.15pm. Mixed, £6 pp/£40 for 8 weeks.
Private tuition: Personalised one-to-one
teaching. £25 ph
Call for further details, or check out
www.clairecarpenter.co.uk/yoga

Esporta
**Balcony level, The Light, The Headrow
(0113) 233 7500**
Membership: discussed after free consulta-
tion. Indoor pool, relaxation room, spa pools,
steam room, sauna, fitness area, gym, aerobics studio, sunbeds, health and beauty
salon, hairdressers.
Mon-Fri 6am-10pm, Sat-Sun 10pm-7pm

LA Fitness
6 Albion Street (0113) 243 3025
Membership: secret (so probably expensive)
Gym, pool, sauna, steam room, jacuzzi, car-
dio room, free weights area, aerobics area.
Mon-Fri 6.30am-10pm,
Sat-Sun 8.30am-7pm

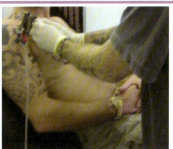

Ultimate Skin Tattoo
29a New Briggate (0113) 244 4940
Friendly, clean, professional and the kind of place that'll give you candid advice before they put needle to skin. An excellent place to go for larger pieces or custom work and if that ain't enough, they also do body piercing.
Tue-Sat 12pm-8pm. From £25

Living Well
Hilton, Neville Street (0113) 244 5443
Membership: £100 joining fee, £42 monthly
Gym, sauna, whirlpool spa, pool, sunbed, cardio vascular room, free towels, toiletries.
Mon-Fri 6.30am-10pm, Sat-Sun 8am-8pm

Virgin Active Life Centre
Cardigan Fields, Kirkstall 0845 130 1555
Membership £48 monthly, £38 off peak
Pool, solarium, sauna, studios, gym, crèche.
Mon-Fri 6am-12pm, Sat-Sun 8am-9pm

Tattoo Parlours/Piercing

Leeds Tattoo & Piercing Studio
4-8 Call Lane (0113) 242 0413
Ear piercing from £9 , Tattoo from £25
Mon-Thu 11am-6pm,
Fri-Sat 10.30am-6pm, Sun 11am-4pm

accommodation

www.itchyleeds.co.uk

Expensive

42 The Calls
42 The Calls (0113) 244 0099
W/day £130-£160, W/end £130 one night, £190 two (room only)

Crowne Plaza
Wellington Street (0113) 244 2200
W/day £130, W/end £110 (b&b)

Hilton
Neville Street (0113) 244 2000
W/day £140 (room only), W/end £78 (b&b)

Malmaison
Sovereign Quay (0113) 398 1000
W/day £110-£125, W/end £79-£125 (room only), breakfast £9.75-£11.75

The Marriott
4 Trevelyan Square (0113) 236 6366
W/day £116+ (room only), W/end £70+ (b&b), breakfast £14.95

Novotel
Whitehall Quay (0113) 242 6446
W/day £105 (room only), W/end £75 (b&b),

Queens Hotel
City Square (0113) 243 1323
W/day max £130, W/end £90 (b&b)

Radisson SAS
The Light, The Headrow (0113) 236 6000
Smooth as you like, if you're ever rich enough to pack up your IKEA sofa and live like a Hollywood star for the rest of your life this would be the place to do it in. Failing that, you can still head here for a weekend of unprecedented luxury. The 147 rooms demonstrate a variety of designs – Italian, Art Deco and Hi-Tech – and there are also excellent bar and conference facilities. With parking and all the facilities The Light has to offer on your doorstep you're pretty much sorted.
W/day & W/end doubles from £110 (b&b)
W/day doubles from £99 (room only)
W/end doubles from £75 (room only)

Radisson SAS Hotel, Leeds

Located in a Grade II Listed Building in the heart of Leeds | 147 Luxury Bedrooms
3 different room styles including Italian, Hi-tech and Art Deco | Exclusive Presidential Suite
8 Meeting Rooms | Video Conferencing, high speed Internet access | Business Centre
The Lounge, a unique dining experience

Quebecs
9 Quebecs Street (0113) 244 8989

If you're looking for pure luxury, this Grade II listed hotel fits the bill perfectly. Each of its 45 guest rooms and suites are decorated in a unique style and contain lots of swish amenities including CD player, music library, satellite TV, personal safe, Egyptian cotton bed linen and complimentary fresh fruit. Victorian in style, it also boasts a restaurant bar and VIP floor – all as decadent as the rest of the building, plus the convenience of its city centre location. Perfect for business and leisure stays alike.

W/day £125+ (room only), w/end £99+ (b&b), full English breakfast £13.50

Mid-Range

Butlers Hotel
40 Cardigan Road (0113) 274 4755
W/end £64.95, W/day £69.95 (b&b)

Golden Lion
2 Briggate (0113) 243 6454

Cracking city centre hotel, that's within seconds of many of the best bars, restaurants, clubs and shops, so you can make the most of your stay. The rooms are well equipped, and

you can go crazy on the helpings at breakfast and they won't bat an eyelid. The attached hotel bar is also remarkable for Leeds by not charging £7 for a pint of Tetley's.
W/end £70, W/day £90 (b&b)

Holiday Inn Express
Cavendish Street (0113) 242 6200
W/end & W/day £67.50 (b&b)

Travel Inn
Wellington Street (0113) 242 8105
W/day £54.95, W/end £49.95 (room only)

Budget

Clock Hotel
317 Roundhay Road (0113) 293 0397
W/end & W/day £20 (room only)

Crescent Hotel
274 Dewsbury Road (0113) 270 1819
W/end & W/day £38 (b&b)

Manxdene Hotel
154 Woodsley Road (0113) 243 2586
W/end & W/day £45 (b&b)

*All prices are correct at time of press. Call ahead for current deals and offers.

GOLDEN LION HOTEL

2 Briggate Leeds
0113 243 6454

laters

www.itchyleeds.co.uk

Late Night Drinking

Leeds is a mecca for late night drinking. Try the Call Lane set – Mojo, Milo, Oporto, Fudge, and Norman for a 2am close. Certified alcoholics can drink until 4am in Oslo.

Cigarettes at 4am?

The Spar garage on Cardigan Road keeps the students in fags and rizlas on a 24 hour basis. GimmeSomeBeer (0113 243 4000) will also deliver cigarettes to your door along with a minimum order of late night booze (can there be a minimum?)

After Hours Fridge Stocking

The Pudsey Asda is available 24hrs for all your late night biscuit needs – Allcotes Shopping Centre, Farley Street (0113) 236 1222.

Food Now!

Lucky's and Milanos are favourite for pizza delivery until 3am, as is Big Mamas in Headingley. Late, late pizza is supplied until 4am by Sicily's. Kashmir will deliver you curries until 3.30am.

Nice Food Now!

Oslo will serve you stylish snacks until closing time, which is 4am at the weekends. The Elbow Room offer the same deal. Nafees will seat you for an Indian meal until 3am in the morning.

Post Club Action/All-Nighters

Casa Loco (19 Lady Lane (0113) 217 1492) dish out techno trance until 6am on a Saturday. Sundissential take up the daytime shift running from 12pm to 12am at Evolution every month. Wander into Hyde Park at the weekend for an open house party or two.

Café Society

Baraka provides late non-alcoholic Moroccan ambience with sheesha pipes, snacks, and fruit teas until past 12am. Kadas does a North African city centre version 'til 1am.

Late Night Shopping

Thursdays is late opening for large department stores – Harvey Nichols, House of Fraser and Debenhams all open until 7pm. The White Rose Centre and Borders both open until 9pm on Thursdays. Mid November sees late night opening until 9pm for most town centre shops until after Christmas.

After Work Beauty Fix

Harvey Nichols and Roberta Mouras will both service your beauty needs until 7pm.

GO TO

Student Sheep for Student Life
www.studentsheep.com

Expo will style your hair into the cutting edge of fashion until 7pm on Thursdays.

Late Night Culture

Leeds Metropolitan University and The Henry Moore Institute both open late on Wednesdays – 7pm and 9pm respectively. Hyde Park Picture House offers weekly late night films.

Other Places

Northern Snooker on Kirkstall stays open until 7am and Grosvenor, Gala, and Napolean Casinos all open until at least 4am. Blue Leopard has performances until 4am.

useful info

travel | useful numbers | takeaway

www.itchyleeds.co.uk

Travel/Useful Numbers

Headingley Limousines
(0113) 293 2733

Forget rocking up to your grad ball or fancy do in your dad's/boyfriend's/mate's battered old motor, arrive in style in a stretch limo from this Headingley based company. Seating eight, the cars are air conditioned and come equipped with bar facilities, plush leather seats, TV, CD and DVD players with surround sound. Expect high quality service,

plus the priceless feeling of pretending you're a film star for the day. In fact, forget the special occasion; just hire one for the day and discover your hidden VIP potential. *£95 for 1 hr, £145 for 2 hrs, £185 for 3hrs, £200 for 4hrs*

Taxis/Private Hire

Taxis
City Cabs....................................(0113) 246 9999
Streamline.................................(0113) 244 3322
Telecabs....................................(0113) 263 7777

Private Hire
Arrow...(0113) 258 0606
Furlongs....................................(0113) 226 7000
Parkways...................................(0113) 274 4441
Pegasus.....................................(0113) 279 9999
Point to Point...........................(0113) 236 0860
Star...(0113) 249 0099
Top Line....................................(0113) 274 1000
Wheels.......................................(0113) 249 9999

STA TRAVEL

ITCHY FEET?

Let STA Travel come to your rescue

If you are itching to discover the world, STA Travel offer it all from low cost flights, accommodation, overland travel, adventure tours, city breaks, round the world & travel insurance to suit every budget.

For bookings call 0870 160 6070 or to find your nearest of 65 UK branches visit our website

www.statravel.co.uk

ABTA
99209

Go on, play away

Go on, play away with National Express and travel at low cost all year round.

If you're aged between 16-25 or a student you can save even more with a National Express Young Persons' Discount Coachcard. Cards cost £10 and give you up to 30% off travel all year.

When booking online you can get hold of your tickets straight away by printing off a National Express e-Ticket, quick, easy and hassle-free.

www.nationalexpress.com

National**Express**

easily the best value

Headingley Limosines

51 St. Chads Drive,
Headingley, Leeds,

0113 293 2723

headingleylimos@aol.com

Bus Companies

Black Prince (local)................... (0113) 252 6033
First Leeds (local)...................... (0113) 244 4321
Metroline (local bus/train)... (0113) 245 7676
National Express...................... (0113) 245 2449
Yorkshire Coastliner............... (0113) 244 8976

Train Companies

GNER.. 08457 225 225
Metroline (local train/bus).... (0113) 245 7676
Midland Mainline...................... 08457 221 125
Arriva.. 0870 602 3322
National Rail Enquiries.............. 08457 484950
Virgin Trains.................................. 08457 222333

Airports

Leeds Bradford.......................... (0113) 250 9696

Manchester............................... (0161) 489 3000

Tourist Info

Leeds City Station Branch..... (0113) 242 5242

Travel Agents

STA
Leeds Uni S.U. (0113) 245 9400
Mon-Fri 10am-6pm
88 Vicar Lane 0870 168 6878
Mon-Fri 9am-6pm (Thu 10am-6pm),
Sat 11am-5pm
182 Woodhouse Lane (0113) 245 8440
Mon-Fri 9.30am-5.30pm (Thu 10am-5.30pm)
National Telesales: 0870 1 600 599
Mon-Thu 9.30am-5.30pm,
Fri-Sat 10.30am-5.30pm

Going places? Under 22?

The new Student Plus MetroCard kicks ass.

For anyone under 22 years old, including full time students.

Useful Numbers

NHS Direct	0845 4647
Childline	0800 11 11
RSPCA	0870 5555 999
Leeds General Infirmary	(0113) 243 2799
St James Hospital	(0113) 243 4144
Samiritans	0845 90 90 90
Rape & Abuse Line	0808 8000 123
Hertz Rent-A-Car	0870 846 0014
Nightline (listening)	(0113) 380 1381
Yorkshire Water Emergency Helpline	0845 124 24 24
British Gas	0800 111 999
City Council	(0113) 234 8080
National Lock & Safe (24hr)	0800 0853637
Police (Non Emergency)	0845 606 0606

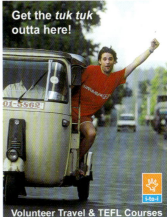

Get the *tuk tuk* outta here!

Volunteer Travel & TEFL Courses
www.i-to-i.com 0870 333 2332

MetroCard offering cheap travel deals to those under 22. Travel information is available online – www.wymetro.com – or by ringing MetroLine on (0113) 245 7676.

West Yorkshire Metro
(0113) 245 7676 www.wymetro.com
Metro monitors and subsidises bus and train services, publishes local travel information and offers some excellent deals on concessionary and prepaid tickets. Choose from weekly, monthly, quarterly or annual MetroCards or the new Student Plus

PIZZAS • BURGERS • DONNERS • BAGUETTE

LUCKYS

FreeFone 0500 11 33 45

FREE DELIVERY

Open 7 days 5pm 'til late

81 Raglan Road
Hyde Park
Leeds LS2 9DZ

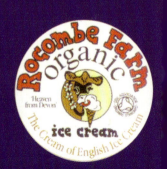

LUXURY ORGANIC ICE CREAM

Takeaway

Tell your mates from down south the price of a margarita from a Leeds pizza joint and they'll gasp in wonder. Explain that this price is for a large and includes delivery and their eyes will narrow in undisguised envy. But who cares if your friends hate you when takeaway is this cheap? Leeds delivers pizzas, curries, and all kinds of burgers cheap as chips. And your mates don't want to know how cheap chips are…

Pizzas/Burgers

Al Capones Pizza
55 New Briggate (0113) 242 5519
Delivers
Mon-Sat 5pm-2am, Sun 5pm-12am

Big Mamas
25 North Lane, Headingley (0113) 274 4899
Delivers
Mon-Sat 5pm-3am

Caesars
209 Stanningley Road (0113) 279 8888
Delivers
Mon-Sun 5pm-12.30am

Dial-a-Pizza
3 Stanmore Hill (0113) 278 5479
Delivers
Sun-Thu 5pm-12.30am, Fri-Sat 5pm-2am

Domino's Pizza
88 Street Lane (0113) 266 4488
Delivers
Sun-Thu 4pm-11pm, Fri-Sat 4pm-12am

Harpos
23 Otley Road (0113) 278 2415
Delivers
Mon-Sun 5pm-12am

Italiano Pizza
109 Chapelton Road (0113) 239 2939
Delivers
Mon-Sun 5pm-4.30am

Luckys
81 Raglan Road 0500 11 33 45
Delivers
Voted best pizza place by students for successive years, you can't beat Lucky's for doing what it does best – a top range of pizzas, and all very cheap. They sell a chocolate pizza, a smoked salmon one, a kebab meat version – these guys are legends.
Mon-Sat 5pm-3am, Sun 5pm-1am

Milanos
79 Raglan Road (0113) 242 5954
Delivers
Mon-Sat 5pm-3am, Sun 5pm-1am

Fish & Chips

Hyde Park Fisheries
12 Hyde Park Corner (0113) 274 7653
No delivery
Mon-Sun 11am-12am

Bretts Fish Restaurant
14 North Lane, Headingley (0113) 232 3344
No delivery, eat in restaurant too
Mon-Fri 12pm-2.30pm & 4.30pm-9pm
Sat 11.30am-9.30pm, Sun 11.30am-8pm

Chinese

Fortune Cookie
81 Raglan Road Hyde Park 08000 155 444
Mighty fine Chinese takeaway. It's tasty, pretty cheap and if you live in the area they'll also deliver for free. Fantastic stuff.
Delivers
Mon-Sat 5pm-2am, Sun 5pm-1am

Sakura
21 North Lane, Headingley (0113) 224 2323
Delivers
Mon-Sun 5pm-12am

Indian

Kashmir
109 Chapeltown Road (0113) 262 5036

Delivers
Mon-Thu 5pm-3.30pm, Fri-Sat 5pm-4.30am,
Sun 5pm-2.30am

Massallas Indian
275 Otley Road (0113) 230 222
Delivers
Mon-Sun 5.30pm-11.30pm

Nafees
69a Raglan Road (0113) 245 3128
No delivery
Mon-Sun 12pm-3am

Nazamz
201 Woodhouse Street (0113) 243 8515
Delivers
Mon-Sun 5pm-2am

Rajput Kebab House
4 St Chads Parade (0113) 278 9008
Delivers
Daily 5pm-3am

Sultans
39 New Briggate (0113) 243 8500
Delivers after 6pm
Mon-Sat 11am-5am, Sun 2pm-12am

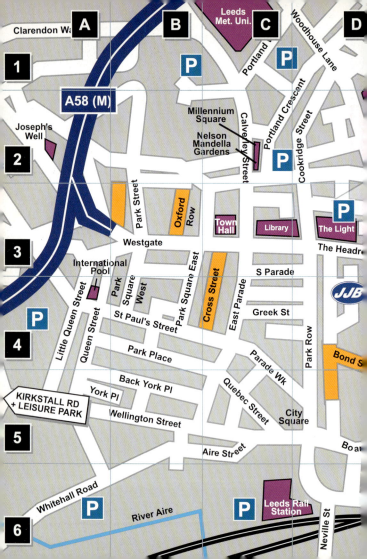

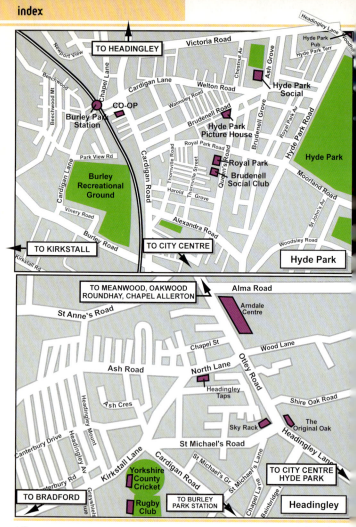

TO HEADINGLEY

Victoria Road

Newport View

Beechwood

Beechwood Mt

Chapel Lane

Cardigan Lane

Welton Road

Walmsley Road

Chestnut Av

Ash Grove

Hyde Park Pub

Hyde Park Terr

Woodho

Headingley Lane

Burley Park Station

CO-OP

Hyde Park Social

Brudenell Road

Hyde Park Picture House

Brudenell Grove

Royal Park Av

Hyde Park Road

Hyde Park

Park View Rd

Cardigan Lane

Cardigan Road

Burley Recreational Ground

Royal Park Road

Thornville Road

Thornville Street

Queen's Road

Royal Park

Brudenell Social Club

Harold

Thornville Grove

Moorland Road

Vinery Road

TO KIRKSTALL

Burley Road

Alexandra Road

St John's Av

Woodsley Road

Kirkstall Rd

TO CITY CENTRE

Hyde Park

TO MEANWOOD, OAKWOOD ROUNDHAY, CHAPEL ALLERTON

Alma Road

Arndale Centre

St Anne's Road

Chapel St

Wood Lane

Otley Road

Ash Road

North Lane

Headingley Taps

Shire Oak Road

Headingley Mount

Ash Cres

The Original Oak

Canterbury Drive

Headingley Av

Sky Rack

Headingley Lane

St Michael's Road

Canterbury Rd

Kirkstall Lane

Cardigan Road

St Michael's Gr

St Michael's Lane

Chapel Lane

Bainbridge

TO CITY CENTRE HYDE PARK

Greyshiel

Yorkshire County Cricket

Rugby Club

TO BRADFORD

TO BURLEY PARK STATION

Headingley

Listing **Page No.**

28 28 Chinese Buffet Menu	23
42 The Calls	124
56 Oriental Restaurant	24
Abbey House Museum	101
Accent	86
Ace	83
After Dark	64
Aire	54
Airports	133
Akbars	19
Alan Cooke	116
Ambienti Design	118
AMF Bowling	110
Angel Inn, The	56
Aqua	86
Arc, The	100
Ark	83
Art's	30
Aspecto	87
Astanga Yoga	122
Atrium	64
Atticus	93
Azendi	94
Baby Jupiter	49
Babylon	11
Baja Beach Club	65
Bar Pacific	46
Bar Phono	65
Barracuda Bar	55
Barratt Homes	112
Bibis	16
Blackwell's	90
Blayde's	76
Blue Leopard	111
Blue Rinse	88
Bondi Beach Bar	99
Borders	90
Box Creative Hair	120

Box, The	53
Brasserie 44	30
brb	118
Break For The Border	54
Bridge, The	76
Brio	17
Browns	11
Bryant Homes	112
Butlers Hotel	126
Café Rouge	15
Cala Homes	112
Calls Grill, The	12
Canton Flavour	23
Carter Jonas	116
Castlehill	116
Cave	118
Chimp	87
Chinese	139
Chino Latino	30
Choonz World-Wide	92
Citrus	32, 109
City Art Gallery	103
City Varieties	98
City Walls	112
Civic Theatre	98
Clock Hotel	127
Clone Zone	79
Club Paradise	66
Cockpit/Rocket	66, 96
Comedy Store, The	100
Cottage Road Cinema	99
Craft Centre	102
Crash	92
Creation	66
Crescent Hotel	127
Crosby Homes	115
Crowne Plaza	124
Cuban Heels	27
Cyberdog	83
Da Mario's	17
Darbar	20
Dark Angel, The	84
Dawn Stretton	86
Diesel	84
Dimitri's	19

Dino's	17
Domane Interiors	118
Dry Dock	34
DV8	111
Edwards	56
Elbow Room, The	36, 67
Elephant Curry Café	20
Envy	87
Esporta	122
Est Est Est	17
Evolution	67
Exit	84
Expo	120
F1 Racing	110
Fab Café	46
Faversham, The	60
Fenton, The	60
Ferret Hall Bistro	12
Fibre	77
Final Curtain, The	88
Firefly	13, 49
Fish & Chips	139
Flannels	84
Flares	69
Fudge	37
Fuji Hiro	24
Futon Company	118
Gala Casino	110
Gieves & Hawkes	87
Global Tribe	94
Golden Lion	126
Granary Wharf	80
Grand Theatre	99
Great Clothes	84
Grosvenor Casino	110
Grove Inn, The	56
Guildford, The	57
Hakuna Matata	37
Handstanned	83
Hansa Gujirati	33
Hard Rock Café	10
Harewood House	105
Harrogate	106
Harvey Nichols	83
Harvey Nichols 4th Floor	12

Headingley Cricket Ground	103
Headingley Lets	59
Headingley Limousines	130
Headingley Taps	61
Heaven and Hell	69
Hendys	116
Henry Moore Institute	103
HiFi	96
HiFi Club	71, 101
Hilton	124
Hip	84
HMV	92
Holiday Inn Express	127
Hollywood Bowl	110
House of Fraser	83
Hunters	116
Hyde Park	61
Hyde Park Social Club	61
Hyena Lounge	101
Ilkley	106
Indian	139
Indonique	118
Jam	120
JJB	94
Jongleurs	101
Joseph	86
Joseph's Well	57, 97
Jumbo	92
Jump	115, 116
Jumpin' Jaks	71
Just Books	90
Kart Skill Leeds	110
Kirkstall Abbey	105
KW Linfoot	115
La Bonavita	18
LA Fitness	122
La Grillade	15
La Tasca	29
Leeds Ind.Museum	102
Leeds Kirkgate Market	83
Leeds Rhinos RLFC	104
Leeds Tattoo & Piercing Studio	123
Leeds Tykes RUFC	104

index

Leodis	14	New Penny, The	77	Reliance, The	15	TKMaxx	83
Library, The	60	No 3 York Place	14	Revolution	42	Toni & Guy	121
Light, The	81	Norman	39	Riley's Pool & Snooker		Tourist Info	133
Lightwater Valley	106	North Bar	52	Club	110	Townhouse, The	44
Little Tokyo	24	Northern Light	14, 39	Robert Mason	118	Train Companies	133
Livebait	29	Northern Snooker C'tre	109	Rock Shack	93	Travel Agents	133
Living Well	123	Novotel	124	Rose & Co	94	Travel Inn	127
LMU	97	O'Neill	85	Roundhay Park	105	Travel/Useful Numbers	130
LMU Theatre	99	O'Neill's	55	Royal Armouries	106	Trio	53
Loft	118	Oasis Hair	121	Royal Park, The	97	Tunnel	86
Lounge Cinema	100	Oasis	86	Sala Thai	29	Ultimate Skin Tattoo	123
LS1	116, 118	Oporto	41	Salts Mill	107	Velvet	78
Lucky Dragon	23	Original Oak, The	61	Salvos	18	Vicky Martin	86
LUU Refectory	97	Out of Step	92	Sandinista!	52	Victoria Commercial Hotel	
Majestyk	71	Oxfam Books	90	Scarborough Hotel	57		56
Malmaison	124	Pack Horse, The	60, 97	Scoot-A-Bout	94	Victoria Quarter, The	80
Manning Stainton	116	Paintball Commando	110	Shabab	20	Virgin Active Life C'tre	123
Manxdene Hotel	127	Park	50	Shogun Teppan-Yaki	24	Virgin Megastore	93
Marriott, The	124	Persimmon Homes	115	Sous Le Nez En Ville	16	Viva Cuba	32
Maxi's		Peter Maturi	118	Space NK	22	Vivienne Westwood	85
Meanwood Valley Urban		Pickerings	118	Spice 4 U	22	Walkabout	55
Farm	105	Pietro	18	Squares	59	Wardrobe, The	32, 45, 74
Millrace, The	25	Pizza Express	18	Ster Century	100	Warehouse	74
Milo	37	Pizzas/Burgers	137	Stick Or Twist	59	Warner Village	100
Mint Club	72	Play Music	92	Stinky's Peephouse	78	Waterstone's	90
Mixing Tin	47	Polar Bear	93	Strand	85	West Park Interiors	118
Modern Hairdressing	120	Pool Court at 42	15	Sugar Shack	88	West Yorkshire Metro	135
Mojo	51	Portafino	18	Takeaway	137	West Yorkshire Playh'se	99
Mook	37	Positively 13 O'Clock	88	Tampopo	25	White Rose Centre, The	80
Morgans City Living	116	Private Hire	130	Tariq's	22	Whitelock's	59
MPV	38	Prohibition	50	Taxis	130	WHSmith	90
Music Zone	92	Proibito	85	Temple Newsham	106	Woodies	62
Nailed On	121	Purple Door, The	111	Teppanyaki	25	XS Hair and Beauty	121
Napoleon Casino	110	Quebecs	126	TGI Fridays	10	York	108
National Martial Arts		Queens Court	78	Thackray Medical		Yorkshire Dales	108
College	104	Queens Hotel	124	Museum	102	Yorkshire Dance	104
National Museum of		Radisson SAS	124	Thai Edge	29	Yorks' Sculpture Park	103
Photography, Film &		Reclaim	42	Think Tank	74	Zara	85
Television	107	Redrow Homes	115	Three Horseshoes	62		
New Inn	61	Rehab	73	Tiger Tiger	32, 49		

More details for all venues can be found on the itchy website

www.itchyleeds.co.uk